baby
SIGN
language

Most Perigee Books are available at special quantity discounts for bulk purchases for sales promotions, premiums, fund-raising, or educational use. Special books, or book excerpts, can also be created to fit specific needs.

For details, write: Special Markets, The Berkley Publishing Group, 375 Hudson Street, New York, New York 10014.

baby SIGN language

for hearing babies

Karyn Warburton

A Perigee Book

THE BERKLEY PUBLISHING GROUP
Published by the Penguin Group
Penguin Group (USA) Inc.
375 Hudson Street, New York, New York 10014, USA
Penguin Group (Canada), 90 Eglinton Avenue East, Suite 700, Toronto, Ontario M4P 2Y3, Canada
(a division of Pearson Penguin Canada Inc.)
Penguin Books Ltd., 80 Strand, London WC2R 0RL, England
Penguin Group Ireland, 25 St. Stephen's Green, Dublin 2, Ireland (a division of Penguin Books Ltd.)
Penguin Group (Australia), 250 Camberwell Road, Camberwell, Victoria 3124, Australia
(a division of Pearson Australia Group Pty. Ltd.)
Penguin Books India Pvt. Ltd., 11 Community Centre, Panchsheel Park, New Delhi—110 017, India
Penguin Group (NZ), Cnr. Airborne and Rosedale Roads, Albany, Auckland 1310, New Zealand
(a division of Pearson New Zealand Ltd.)
Penguin Books (South Africa) (Pty.) Ltd., 24 Sturdee Avenue, Rosebank, Johannesburg 2196, South Africa

Penguin Books Ltd., Registered Offices: 80 Strand, London WC2R 0RL, England

While the author has made every effort to provide accurate telephone numbers and Internet addresses at the time of publication, neither the publisher nor the author assumes any responsibility for errors, or for changes that occur after publication. Further, publisher does not have any control over and does not assume any responsibility for author or third-party websites or their content.

BABY SIGN LANGUAGE

First American edition: July 2006
Previously published in New Zealand in 2004 by Baby Talk Limited.

Perigee trade paperback ISBN: 0-399-53260-9

An application to register this book for cataloging has been submitted to the Library of Congress.

PRINTED IN THE UNITED STATES OF AMERICA

10 9 8 7 6 5 4 3 2 1

PUBLISHER'S NOTE: Information in this book is developed from the author's experiences and observations, the experiences of Baby Talk families, and from public information and educational sources. No claim is made or warranty given as to the results achievable by using the information contained in this book. Neither the author nor Baby Talk Limited shall have or accept any liability or responsibility to any person or entity with respect to the results of the book's suggested techniques.

For my daughter, Isabella, and all the children I have worked with during my years as a Montessori teacher and nanny, without whom we would not have discovered this wonderful early communication tool. They really taught me a lot!

Isabella (14 months old) signs HAIRBRUSH

Acknowledgments

I would like to thank all the families who contributed their stories, photographs and ideas to make this book possible. A special thank-you to Ulrike Gaul and Sharon and Ashleigh Eastwood for sharing their stories.

My husband, Giles, deserves a large amount of recognition for his hard work piecing this book together and for his endless support, encouragement and computer skills. Thank you for sharing all the long nights with me.

I am eternally grateful to our editor, Graham Adams, for his time and guidance when it came to knocking my manuscript into shape, and to Kylie Penman for the many hours put in helping with layout and designing the original cover, then redesigning it when we frequently changed our minds!

"Communication is not simply about using words with meaning; to a baby who does not have the skills to talk, communication is about signs."

—Dorothy Einon

Author of *Early Learning* and lecturer at University College, London

Foreword

By Gordon Dryden
Coauthor of *The Learning Revolution*

By now the lessons should be engraved in the mind of every young parent: Around 50 percent of the ability to learn is developed in the first four to five years of life—not 50 percent of one's wisdom, knowledge or intelligence, but around half of the most vital pathways in the brain, the pathways on which all other learning will be based.

This means parents, and not professionals, are the world's most important teachers. And home is the most important school.

Maria Montessori, the great Italian educator, was proving it in practice around a hundred years ago. By providing the right multisensory environment, she had hundreds of three- and four-year-olds reading, writing and doing basic mathematics well before starting school.

Now Karyn Warburton adds another great insight into early childhood knowledge: baby sign language — even before children can speak and walk.

Her practical experience as a mother and a teacher bears out some of the latest findings of neuroscience. We know, for instance, that babies can absorb and store information by sight and sound well before they can crawl or walk. Very simply that is because of the way in which the nerve pathways around the brain and the body are myelinated — by the insulating sheath that grows around those pathways. And the brain's incoming pathways are myelinated before the long motor pathways that enable young legs to walk. And the speech pathways in the forebrain are myelinated after the segments of the brain that process seeing and hearing.

But you don't have to be a brain scientist to know that we learn better and faster if we use all our senses. The more babies can see, hear, feel, smell and taste experience, the more they learn. And the more they can physically play with information, the faster and more effective their learning. Right throughout life: if you want to learn it, do it!

Now Karyn Warburton's fine book provides a completely new dimension to this basic knowledge. In short: a great communications tool that not only encourages babies to absorb information right from the start — but to play with it, act on it, and enjoy it.

Better still, it's easy. And it's fun.

Contents

Contents

Chapter 8 Signing Dictionary 79

Welcome

You are about to embark on one of the most rewarding experiences you and your baby will share together during their most formative years.

Since we began running baby signing workshops in early 2001, thousands of parents have integrated the use of Baby Talk baby sign language into their daily lives. As working parents ourselves, we understand just how hectic life can be, leaving limited time available to learn a new skill. That is why our approach to learning baby sign language is to keep the entire process as simple, natural and straightforward as possible, not to mention FUN.

Karyn & Isabella

Baby signing is an experience that no parent and child should miss out on!

About the Author

Karyn Warburton, the founder of Baby Talk, is a Montessori preschool teacher with more than 14 years experience with young children. Karyn has studied and worked in the field of childcare in both New Zealand and the United Kingdom, where she incorporated the use of sign language in her work with special needs children, children with English as a second language and preverbal infants. Karyn's own daughter, Isabella, was an enthusiastic baby signer.

About This Book

We have huge numbers of parents approaching us wanting our workshop to be available in book form. Most had read other baby sign language books in the past but could not find any that offered good, clear instruction and inspiring examples. The other common request was for a signing dictionary that contained a broad selection of important signs. With this in mind we created *Baby Sign Language.*

Chapters one and two briefly look at the theory surrounding baby sign language and touch on some important research carried out to date and the many benefits that were discovered. We feel it is important that parents are aware of the origins of baby sign language for hearing babies and understand how it assists with their infant's development.

Chapters three to five cover the all important practical aspects of how to teach baby sign language to your baby. The "Getting Started" section tells you exactly that—when to get started, which signs to begin with, how to teach these signs and what these first signs might look like. There is also a troubleshooting area for the most common problems experienced by signing parents.

Chapter eight contains our extended sign dictionary, which includes words our signing families and childcare providers have found the most useful. We have categorized each set of signs to make them easier to locate. We have also graded each sign — beginner 0–9 months, intermediate 10–13 months and advanced 14 months and over — which will allow parents to select the signs that are best suited to their own baby's abilities.

All topics have been developed using current research, our own experiences and observations, and those of the thousands of parents and caregivers who have attended our workshops. Happy signing!

How to Use This Book

We have included numerous stories from signing parents who have attended our classes, and these are highlighted in gray boxes throughout the book.

The following symbols point out important factors to be aware of, areas where you may need to do some preparation and areas to avoid.

This symbol indicates important factors to be aware of when learning to sign.

This symbol indicates that there are exercises that you can follow to help with teaching your signs.

This symbol highlights the things that we suggest you avoid in teaching your signs.

The above are intended as guidelines, based on our own experiences and the feedback from thousands of parents who have attended Baby Talk workshops. For more help, visit www.baby-talk.com.

Chapter 1

What Is Baby Sign Language?

Baby Sign Language

Baby sign language is a collection of simple, easy-to-remember gestures that your *hearing* baby can use to communicate with you until they master spoken language.

All babies instinctively use their body language, facial expressions, noises, cries and non-verbal gestures in order to communicate with you. Baby sign language is simply an extension of what your baby is already doing. Until a baby is able to tell you their needs verbally, their need to "signal" physically is extremely important. For example, a 10-month-old baby can make a few interesting noises in order to gain your attention or to show pleasure, excitement and distaste. This very same baby is able to convey many more ideas to you by using physical gestures and body movements — waving good-bye, raising his arms to be picked up, flapping his arms and legs to show excitement, smacking his lips when offered food, spitting food out or refusing to open his mouth when he has had enough or doesn't like his food. He can tell you when he wants an object by pointing to it or reaching for it and will pass objects to you as part of a game or to initiate an interaction or conversation. He is easily able to demonstrate anger by arching his back, clenching his fists and turning purple!

Child development experts, parents and caregivers around the world are beginning to recognize just how important these nonverbal gestures are in the early stages of language development and understanding.

By expanding your baby's own repertoire of gestures he will be able to tell you exactly what he wants using one simple movement, whether it's more <u>milk</u>, a <u>biscuit</u> or just to tell you about a <u>bird</u> he has seen in a <u>tree</u>, instead of resorting to the usual crying, grunting and pointing. This eliminates a huge amount of stress and anxiety for both parent and child, and opens up an exciting new world of pre-verbal communication.

"In a spoken language environment a baby's gestures are not seen as particularly significant, whereas in a signing environment they are credited with the status of first words" (Nicola Grove, 1986, Makaton Vocabulary Development Project).

Isabella (10 months old) signs MORE

Christmas is always a special time of year in our household. Since the arrival of our son, Jack (now 15 months old), it is even more exciting. I love to watch him as he stares with absolute delight at our Christmas tree, laden with decorations and brightly colored lights. This year Jack was insistent with his offers to "help" when it came time to decorate our home and our Christmas tree. We decided it would be a nice surprise to have it all done before Daddy came home from work. Jack couldn't wait to show his father and was waiting somewhat impatiently for his arrival. As soon as Daddy stepped foot inside the door, Jack led him by the hand to the tree. Amidst the "ooohs and ahhhs" as we all marveled at the beautiful tree, Jack began shouting, "Dat, dat," pointing to the power switch beside the tree and blinking his eyes furiously. His father dutifully switched it on and immediately the lights on the tree began to flash on and off. From that point on, if Jack wanted the lights to be turned on he would simply look at you and madly blink his eyes — we knew exactly what he was after! — Melanie, Auckland, New Zealand

Studies have shown that babies aged between 6 and 30 months benefit the most from using baby sign language. Babies born prematurely, children learning a second language and those experiencing speech delays have also benefited immensely. Some hospitals and caregivers even use the system with stroke victims and other patients who are temporarily unable to speak.

The Baby Talk Program

The gestures we use are *based* on signs used within the deaf community. The difference is that spoken words are **ALWAYS** used in conjunction with the signs, and signs are used in correct speech order — unlike most signing systems for the deaf. Because young babies have limited coordination and dexterity, we have substituted some of the more difficult signs, or those requiring a two-symbol combination, with simplified gestures. This enables a baby to make use of these signs from a much earlier age. Baby sign language is intended to be an aid to early communication, **NOT** a second language. Signs do not have to be as precise as is required in signing systems such as American Sign Language (ASL) and British Sign Language (BSL), whereby a slight alteration to a movement can change the meaning of a sign entirely. It also does not matter to your baby whether you are left- or right-handed, as your baby will naturally use their dominant hand to perform signs.

The Baby Talk approach encourages parents to sign only the most important words in their speech, initially only emphasizing one word in each sentence. This makes it easier for your infant to work out what it is you are talking about, by isolation and repetition. The signs we have included in our dictionary relate to objects, feelings and concepts that are of interest to young children. Focusing on what your baby enjoys, and would most likely want to talk to you about, will ensure success at signing.

We strongly encourage incorporating the use of games, songs, toys, books and outings into the learning process, to make the whole experience as enjoyable as possible for you and your baby.

The sign suggestions we have included in our dictionary are purely that. Busy parents found it much easier to have ready-made signs available to them and preferred to work with gestures that had been tried and tested with young babies. You can use any signing system you like, just be mindful of your baby's physical and cognitive capabilities when choosing signs, and don't be afraid to create your own. Also, be open to your baby's own inventions and incorporate these into your signing vocabulary.

Whichever signing system you use, the way you introduce them to your baby is the same.

 Teaching your infant to sign should never be forced, and your child should never be made to feel pressured at any time.

Please Note: If you intend to teach your baby to sign as a second language, we strongly recommend that you attend the appropriate courses in your native sign language before you begin. As with any new language, it can take several years to become proficient, and you will need to stay several steps ahead of your baby.

A Brief History of Sign Language

Sign language has been used by both hearing and deaf communities around the world for centuries. Michael C. Corballis, a professor of psychology at the University of Auckland, New Zealand, and author of the book *From Hand to Mouth: The Origins of Language*, believes that speech evolved from the use of physical gestures or "sign language." Early man relied heavily upon nonverbal gestures in order to communicate and gradually began to produce vocal sounds to accompany signs. The ability to produce autonomous speech did not develop until approximately 50,000 years ago, which is much later than was previously thought.

Sign language has continued to be a very useful tool for the hearing over the ages. For example, records dating back to before the 16th century show that Benedictine monks used a form of sign language to communicate when they observed long periods of silence.

In 1853, David Bartlett was teaching deaf children and their hearing siblings in a family school. He began to notice how using sign language with hearing children was having a positive effect on their early language development. Unfortunately, around the same time, attitudes began to change and the use of sign language for the deaf as well as the hearing was strongly discouraged in favor of the "speech method" (using the voice and lip-reading) of communication. As a result, interest in studying the benefits of signing with hearing children faded.

It is only in the last two decades that researchers have rediscovered the great many benefits hearing babies gain from using a simple series of nonverbal gestures now universally called baby sign language.

Research on Baby Sign Language

Child development expert and coauthor of *Baby Signs* Linda Acredolo, PhD, observed her 12-month-old daughter creating and using symbolic gestures in order to communicate with her. At that stage little research had been undertaken into what appears to be an innate process and an integral part of a child's fledgling attempts at preverbal communication.

Linda and her research partner, Susan Goodwyn, PhD, wondered what would happen if parents were to purposefully introduce more signs to their babies. So began a study that would span more than 20 years. The most recognized and best-known piece of research carried out by the two professors is outlined below.

Results of the Two-Year Study

In 1989 Linda and Susan began a government-funded study involving more than 100 families with 11-month-old babies. Each family participating in the study was required to fit certain criteria, ensuring that those taking part were at an equivalent stage at the beginning. This included factors such as English being the only language spoken within the home, family income and education, the sex and birth order of the child, and their vocalization skills.

One third of the families were shown how to use "baby signs." Another third were instructed to use a language intervention program, which encouraged parents to model spoken words on a more regular basis than they would otherwise. The remaining families were the control group and were to continue caring for their babies as normal. None of these groups was aware of the other participants and their role in the study.

The idea was to follow the progress of each family and, after a two-year period, test for any side effects or benefits — positive or negative, in the babies who were using signs.

Results of the Complete Study

The babies who used signs outperformed the nonsigners in every comparison:

- *Scored higher on intelligence tests.*
- *Understood more words.*
- *Had larger vocabularies.*
- *Engaged in more sophisticated play.*

The parents of the signing babies also noted other advantages:

- *Increased communication.*
- *Decreased frustration and fewer tantrums.*
- *Enriched parent-infant bond.*
- *Increased self-confidence.*
- *Greater interest in books.*

Study on Long-Term Benefits

The researchers returned to visit the families who participated in their earlier study. The babies, then eight years old, were tested to see if there were any long-term benefits. It was found that the children who used signs as infants had an average IQ of 114 compared with 102 for their nonsigning counterparts.

It was also discovered that the children who used signs in their early language development also showed an above-average understanding of the English language. Because the signing babies were able to practice using language long before they were able to speak, their understanding of English language and syntax was more advanced.

Other Leading Research

Dr. Marilyn Daniels, author of *Dancing With Words: Signing for Hearing Children's Literacy* and associate professor of speech communication at Pennsylvania State University, is probably the most recognized authority and dedicated researcher studying the benefits of teaching sign language to hearing children, from preschool through to sixth-grade level.

As well as observing the benefits cited by Drs. Acredolo and Goodwyn in their study of 11-month-old babies, Dr. Daniels took her studies further to include older hearing children and discovered even more significant advantages. She paid particular attention to children who had a history of learning difficulties, particularly in areas such as vocabulary retention, reading and spelling.

Teachers taking part in these studies began to incorporate the use of sign language into their curricula. Children who were previously struggling in fundamental areas of their education began to show great improvement, and in most cases vocabulary was increased by 15 to 20 percent. Teachers found that not only did the children in their classes enjoy the new activity, but discovered that using this multisensory approach (auditory, visual and kinetic) actually accelerated the children's learning ability.

Dr. Daniels expanded her research and began to investigate the effects of using sign language to teach children to read. Several of her graduate students observed that hearing children with deaf parents were excelling in this area, and in most cases these children were able to read before they began school. Schools taking part in this new study introduced the manual alphabet, which is used by the deaf community for fingerspelling.

Children were taught the individual sounds for each letter of the alphabet in conjunction with the written symbol and the associated sign. In an earlier study, McNight (1979) found that "It is easier to connect the visual letter to a manual sign, and then to a verbal sound, than it was to go directly to the verbal sound." At a later stage children were shown how to spell phonetic words by fingerspelling the individual letters alongside the letter sounds and written symbols.

Nonphonetic words were signed and spoken as a whole, as sight words. With repetition the children were soon able to recall the new vocabulary and were also able to figure out new words by themselves. Teachers found that the children gained huge confidence from their new ability, which in turn made them more enthusiastic to progress further.

Because of the great results they received, not just academically but also in improving the children's self-esteem, the schools involved in Dr. Daniels's research went on to implement the program permanently once the study concluded.

Kaleb signs HOT

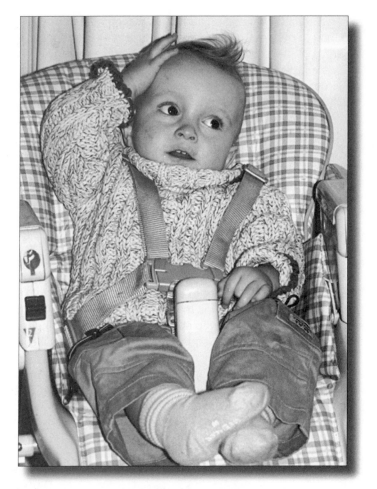

Oscar signs CRAZY

Oscar used his sign for <u>crazy</u> to tell his mother just what he thought of his doctor when told he was too young to comprehend and use sign language as a form of early communication.

Chapter 2

Why Teach Your Baby to Sign?

The Benefits

It's Fun!

There are so many good reasons for introducing your child to the world of baby signing, but most of all, signing is fun. From the moment you see your baby repeat their first sign, you will be hooked.

Babies love signing because it gives them a means to connect with you more often and about many different things that they would otherwise be unable to convey.

The best part is that there are hundreds of opportunities every day to teach signs!

Bright Sparks — Building Knowledge

As a signing parent you become increasingly aware of just how much your baby is capable of understanding. You spend more time interacting and talking to your baby about a wider variety of subjects. Your baby is able to take charge of his own education by indicating to you with a simple gesture just what it is he would like to know more about. He will also become very skillful at extracting further information from you!

Isabella had learned the sign for <u>hat</u> quite early on (around 10 months). She felt very confident she knew what a hat was and would point out hats whenever she saw one. One day she came across somebody wearing headphones. Isabella had not seen headphones before and was curious as to what they were. She turned to me and signed <u>hat</u> with a quizzical look on her face. She knew it wasn't like any hat she had seen before and seemed to be looking for clarification by using what she knew of "things that go on the head." I quickly made up a sign for headphones and told her what they were for. Isabella seemed perfectly happy about my explanation and filed away the information. She had learned a new concept and a new sign, without the ability to say any of the relevant words!
— Karyn Warburton

Baby sign language is a useful tool for assisting your baby in his development of concepts. Babies learn to form concepts by their experiences and are continually refining their ideas and understanding. Infants start with "the big picture" and work from there. For example, when a baby first encounters a creature with four legs, a tail and fur, and is told it is a cat, suddenly every animal that loosely resembles a cat falls into the same category. This is because *cat* is the only word they may have learned to date to identify an animal. Likewise, for a while all men are "Daddy." It isn't until a baby has more experiences that they are able to clarify their ideas and put these new revelations into the correct "boxes" in their minds.

Yesterday while Jared was doing a puzzle with me he was pointing out all the animals and either signing or saying what they were. When he got to lion he wasn't sure what it was, and signed and said <u>cat</u> — so I showed him the <u>lion</u> sign and roared. He caught on really quickly and that night proudly showed Dad his lion on the puzzle with the correct sign and sound. I've just today looked up the sign for <u>tiger</u> because last night while reading *Spot Goes to the Circus* he knew the difference between a tiger and a lion — he only signed and roared for the <u>lion</u> — so tonight we'll add <u>tiger</u> to his repertoire! — Colleen, Napier, New Zealand

I See What You Mean — Making Words Visual

Signs give meaning to words that would otherwise be too abstract for your baby to comprehend until they were much older. The word *wind*, for example, does not refer to something your baby can see, but using an iconic gesture makes the subject instantly understood. The same can be said for talking about emotions and feelings. Dr. Daniels likens signing to "making word pictures in the air." Unlike a spoken word, a sign can be held static for a baby to imitate.

My son Robert is 13 months old and understands a few signs but only signs <u>lion</u> himself. Last week in the car he was frantically signing <u>lion</u> and making a roaring sound. I looked where he was looking and saw a pile of autumn leaves we had picked up in the park. It did look like a lion's mane! It would be years before he could share that with me using speech. Bob is obsessed in his own little toddler way with lions and each time we go to the local zoo he starts signing <u>lion</u> as soon as we arrive at the car park. He will not look at anything until we get to the lions and he has said hello to them all. Without the signing we would have thought he hated going to the zoo or was bored, when actually the opposite is true, he just likes to start with the lions. — Julie, Christchurch, New Zealand

Bathed in Language — A Greater Understanding

A baby who is immersed in spoken language (accompanied by sign language) naturally has a greater understanding of words and concepts. When your baby uses a sign to tell you about something that is of interest to him, you instinctively give him more information. For example, "Oh, you can see a <u>cat</u>. Yes, there it is, sitting on the fence. What a beautiful, big, black <u>cat</u> it is. What do you think he is looking at?" and so on. As a result your baby hears more spoken words in a relaxed and natural way.

A Walking Thesaurus — Building Larger Vocabularies

Signing babies are not reliant on waiting until they have enough spoken words at their disposal in order to begin the communication process — they are able to use their signs in the interim. At the age of 12 months, Isabella had a collection of 10 spoken words and used 25 signs, giving her a vocabulary of 35 "words" for objects or needs she wanted to tell us about. Twins Megan and Louise both had 6 spoken words and 15 signs at the same age. Just to show that boys are equally as clever, Thomas (11 months old) could say 4 words and had a signing vocabulary of 12 words.

At the age of two, the children taking part in Drs. Acredolo and Goodwyn's study had their vocabularies tested. It was found that the signing babies had 50 more spoken words than the nonsigners, and at three had a vocabulary equivalent to that of most four-year-olds.

The ability to form simple sentences using a combination of signs and words, or signs on their own, in most cases begins at a much earlier age. For example, at the age of 11 months, Zoe began to sign <u>Mummy where?</u>, <u>Mummy bye-bye</u> and <u>pacifier where?</u>; Megan, 12 months, would sign <u>more milk</u>, <u>more book</u>, <u>food finished</u> and <u>bath finished</u> as she watched the water go down the drain.

These babies began this process at least 6 months earlier than the expected 18 to 24 months. This was possible because these babies had the ability to "name" objects and ideas by using their nonverbal gestures from a very young age, and forming sentences was the next natural step. This is a giant leap in a baby's cognitive development.

By giving your baby this skill you really are giving them a natural head start with their learning!

> At 15 months of age my daughter had learned most of the animal signs in your resource guide. She had even made up her own signs for <u>moose</u> and <u>ibix</u>, which completely blew me away! Even our family doctor couldn't believe how advanced she was, so he performed the Denver Developmental Test on her and found her cognitive skills to be equivalent to those of a 30-month-old. The doctor didn't believe the results so he repeated the test and the results were the same!
> — Robin, Waitakere City, New Zealand

Let's Pretend — Learning Through Role Playing

Signing babies begin to take part in role-playing games at an earlier age. This is mainly due to the fact that signing parents have realized just how much their babies are capable of learning. As a result, they interact with their infants more, and on a more advanced level. Babies also become much more observant and begin to watch everything you do — they then re-create their observations and use them in their role-playing games.

Isabella was able to pretend at around the age of 13 months. I observed her at play one afternoon. She had her favorite teddy bear and a bowl and seemed to be searching for something else to use in her game. Eventually she came across a pen. Isabella then proceeded to feed her teddy imaginary food using the pen as a spoon. This may not sound very startling, but the ability to represent objects using something not intended for that purpose is a big step in a child's intellectual development. As far as I can remember, I never fed Isabella with a pen and I am fairly sure her father hasn't! — Karyn Warburton

Listen Up! — More Communication Attempts

A baby who can successfully communicate an idea or need to their parent or caregiver experiences so much personal satisfaction in having done so that they try again and again to achieve the same result. It is almost as if they become addicted to the communication process!

Yesterday we were out in a place Benjamin didn't know, and he started signing where. This morning, Andrew was taking him out of our room and he started signing come, which he repeated every time I stopped and asked him if he wanted me to come. An hour later, he was playing in his room and I asked him to come with me, using the sign at the same time. He grinned and shook his head, which he has never done before. So I said again to come with me, and he grinned again and signed come to me! I think communication has begun. — Robyn, Auckland, New Zealand

Cool, Calm and Collected — Reduced Frustration

Being less frustrated really goes hand in hand with being able to clearly express yourself. A child who does not use signs to communicate will still attempt to get their message across any way possible. Because different areas of the brain are used for understanding and for speaking, babies know what they want to say but, until they are able to speak, have no easy means to tell you what is on their minds. Unfortunately, their early attempts generally take the form of grunting, pointing and whining, which eventually leads to tears and anger when you don't understand them. There is nothing more frustrating than not being understood — at any age!

I just thought I'd let you know that Mackenzie is now using 18 signs, and she understands 25 in total. Colin and I are thrilled with her progress. Because it has become second nature, we sign wherever we are and people who have noticed have been very impressed, not just by Mackenzie's signing but by her behavior too. She is 13 months old now and is seldom frustrated or unhappy, and I'm sure it's because she knows how to make herself understood. — Pauline, Auckland, New Zealand

We Make a Great Team — Building a Strong Relationship

A family that signs together grows and learns together! Becoming a parent is a truly amazing experience. It is fascinating to observe these tiny individuals as they grow and develop their own little personalities. When you introduce a simple signing system it is wonderful to watch as your baby's language skills develop. Instead of being a passive little bundle observing family discussions and waiting to be included, they begin to take an active role using their newfound skill and even initiate conversations by themselves. As a result, you begin to learn so much more about each other, and from a much younger age. Your baby doesn't need to know hundreds of signs, and even small steps forward in communicating can make a significant difference to your relationship with your infant. Also, having fewer tantrums is a real bonus in the bonding process. This allows for many more positive experiences for everyone.

Adam is doing well with his signs and tells me when the <u>cat</u> wants to <u>eat</u> and when it has <u>finished</u>. He also told me to <u>finish</u> in the garden as he had had enough. Adam tried out all his signs to get out of going to bed, but Mummy won with the <u>sleep</u> sign. — Kerryn, Auckland, New Zealand

A Gentle Reminder

Signing can also be a great way to discreetly jog a child's memory. Instead of intervening and saying out loud, "Don't forget to say thank you!" or shouting, "Do you need the toilet?" across a crowded room, you can simply sign <u>thank you</u> or <u>toilet</u> to your child — saving them a great deal of embarrassment. Baby sign language also allows you to reprimand a child from a distance without needing to draw any unnecessary attention to them or their behavior.

Aren't I Great! — A Confident Child

A baby who is able to freely communicate begins to feel more confident in his own ability, and not just in signing. Signing babies develop a really positive attitude and become very eager to learn as much as they can about their world. They also seem more willing to try a new activity, even if they know it may be too difficult for them.

A self-assured child is more likely to stand up for himself and is less likely to be bullied at school.

Garth, a 16-month-old boy who attends my daycare center, was an extremely shy and uncertain child. He would suck his thumb and play with his ear whenever he felt uncomfortable or threatened (which was a lot of the time!). His shyness meant he wouldn't speak to anyone, which made it difficult for everyone, not just himself. When we began to introduce baby sign language, the whole situation changed. After just a few days Garth walked up to me, he didn't make eye contact, but I could clearly see him using the sign for <u>diaper change</u>. When I responded to his request he was openly excited with his achievement. As time went on, the more signs we taught, the more confident Garth became. He gradually began to open up more, he started smiling and laughing and has now given up sucking his thumb altogether. Garth will now stand up for himself and has become more assertive of his rights. It is plainly visible just how much more comfortable and secure Garth feels in his environment now that he is able to tell everyone what he wants. — Ulrike, Rotorua, New Zealand

Help Me Do It By Myself — Becoming More Independent

The fact that your baby feels confident in his ability to tell you what he wants, when he wants it, gives him a greater sense of independence. Because he has a greater understanding of his environment, and because he has another means of learning, associating and understanding, he will feel freer to explore. You are providing a "scaffolding" for your baby's learning experiences, whereby your baby makes new discoveries knowing you are there for support and encouragement. If he needs help along the way he is easily able to ask for it.

I have been signing flat out to Madeline, and she loves it. When we started, just after your course here in Tauranga, she was eight months old, it took about six weeks till she signed back, but once she clicked on to it she hasn't looked back. Now she picks up a new sign in a day. She is now one year old and can sign <u>eat</u>, <u>drink</u>, <u>milk</u>, <u>cat</u>, <u>fish</u>, <u>all finished</u>, <u>more</u>, <u>shoes</u>, <u>hat</u>, <u>hairbrush</u>, <u>toothbrush</u>, <u>home</u>, <u>diaper change</u>, <u>music</u>, <u>dog</u> and many others. Madeline also understands others that she doesn't actually sign herself. She is so proud of herself when she signs for things, and it makes it so easy for us when she asks for something using her signs. I have been recommending it to everyone I know!! — Suzie, Tauranga, New Zealand

More Books Please! — Develop an Early Love of Reading

Sitting quietly and reading books with a signing baby moves story time to a whole new level. They begin to pay closer attention to the pictures and can take a more interactive role in the reading process. They even begin to "read" books to you, by pointing out the objects they recognize and using the signs, words or sounds for them. Reading together is such a lovely relaxed time and your baby feels very secure snuggled up next to you. This is also an ideal time for your little one to learn more signs.

We found books with clear, uncluttered pictures to be an ideal resource for teaching new signs. With the babies I have cared for I would estimate that approximately 60 percent of the signs learned were introduced this way.

Parents have also noticed that their signing babies develop excellent memories and become more observant and curious and are better able to concentrate on a task, all of which are necessary skills for reading. The improved dexterity and co-ordination they experience as a result of signing as youngsters goes a long way to help with their writing skills later on as well.

> I want to encourage anyone out there who is unsure if they should use signing, it's a beautiful thing to be able to sit with an 11-month-old and read a book as they sign the names of the animals in the story! — Bridget, Wellington, New Zealand

Isabella (14 months old) signs FLOWER

Language Development and Sign Language

How a Baby Acquires Language

Babies are very adept when it comes to learning about language, and you would be amazed at how much they can comprehend. Your baby first learns to understand spoken language by picking out key words in your speech. He slowly begins to realize that these verbal symbols stand for physical objects and later moves on to learning about more intangible ideas and feelings. Your baby relies a great deal on visual clues, such as observing your body language and facial expressions as well as the sounds you are making when deciphering what it is you are saying to him.

The Mechanics of It

The actual physical task of producing spoken language is a very complex activity for your baby. Many fine-motor skills in the mouth and throat need to be perfected and coordinated before the exact sounds required in spoken language can be recreated. Your baby practices endlessly, generating an assortment of entertaining noises, usually when you want him to go to sleep! By doing this he is learning how his mouth works and is exercising and gaining control over his tongue, vocal cords, breathing and the muscles in his throat — all necessary skills for producing speech. A baby's language development is highly individual, but follows a general sequence roughly like this:

1 to 2 months	Cries vigorously with a variable pitch. Produces involuntary movements and facial expressions. Coos, fusses and cries when distressed. Can recognize mother's voice (from one week). Upset by loud noises. Can express rage.
3 months	Cries when annoyed or uncomfortable. Can vocalize and produce some vowel sounds. Will show excitement when he hears familiar sounds. Will smile to express pleasure.
4 to 5 months	Experiments with different sounds and produces some consonants. Can mimic facial and lip movements. Learns about turn-taking during your conversations with him. Will begin to imitate sounds.
6 to 7 months	Learns that conversations use sounds and will begin to add noises to his interactions. Will begin to babble, using first single and then double syllables. Combines vowels and consonants and "speaks" to himself in a sing-song tone. Will laugh out loud, yell, whisper and blow raspberries.
7 to 9 months	Has worked out that your conversations with him convey information. **He begins to spontaneously create nonverbal gestures** in order to "tell" you about his own thoughts. Babbling rises and falls and sounds more like real conversation. Can imitate adult noises like a shout or cough and will shout to get attention. Can express anger, fear and joy. Understands "no" and "bye-bye."

10 months	Imitates pitch and may say one recognizable word. Can now comprehend several simple words. (Deaf babies typically make their first sign at this age.) May begin to point and use more self-created signs.
1 year	Babbles continuously like conversation, uses most vowels and many consonants, attempts to mimic words and sounds. May bring things of interest to you or lead you to objects they want.

 DON'T PANIC! — Please keep in mind that some infants are much slower than this timetable and this by no means indicates that your baby is falling behind. It may just be that they are more interested in other areas of their development at this stage. If you are concerned about your baby's progress in any area, consult your doctor or health professional to dispel any worries.

A fascinating study involving a group of deaf toddlers who were taught to use sign language at a very young age discovered that the toddlers, in most cases, learned at a quicker rate than their hearing contemporaries. The vocabularies of the deaf children were far greater than those of the hearing children at the same age, because the children who could hear had to wait until they could verbalize words in order to enjoy the same amount of communication "freedom." It can take 18 to 24 months for a hearing child to produce enough spoken words to create simple sentences. A baby who is taught to sign does not have to wait until their speech is mature enough to be understood — they can take part in conversations from a much earlier age.

Garth signs ELEPHANT

Why Do Signing Babies Speak Earlier?

Every healthy, unimpeded baby is able to produce spoken language — it is what they were born to do! In fact, in multilingual households, babies can easily learn more than one language.

A Multisensory Experience

Babies use their whole bodies to explore their environment and learn by using their senses. So it makes perfect sense to use a "hands on" way of introducing language. By teaching your child to use baby sign language you are stimulating his brain development with much greater effect by giving him three modes of input.

1. AUDITORY — he can hear how the spoken word sounds.

2. VISUAL — your baby can "see" the word when you show him the corresponding sign. He also watches your facial expression, body language and mouth shape in order to see how the word is formed when spoken.

3. KINETIC — the repetitive physical movement involved in reproducing a sign helps to create a more lasting impression in your baby's memory of both the sound of the word and the concept behind it. We all know that babies (not to mention most adults) learn best by doing.

> On a drive up the coast one weekend with my partner and baby (then 15 months old) I noticed her signing something to me. She was repeatedly using two separate signs simultaneously and pointing out of the window. I couldn't believe my eyes when I realized what she was doing — she didn't have a sign for beach as yet so was signing sand and water. — Robyn, Auckland, New Zealand

Monkey See, Monkey Do!

Babies observe people all around them using spoken language and strive to take part in these pleasant exchanges. Being very social creatures, babies will use any means possible to connect with other human beings. Using signs is a terrific way to achieve this and is a wonderful precursor to speech. However, you will find that as your baby develops they will feel the need to communicate their ideas at a much faster rate than is possible with signs and discover that they don't have a sign for everything they want to convey. They also want to broaden their social circle to include "nonsigners." This is when your child begins to outgrow baby sign language and speech starts to take over.

Say That Again?

When you are introducing signs to your baby you are inclined to speak more slowly and deliberately. You also tend to repeat a sentence more than once. This way, your baby is given more opportunities to hear the individual sounds, and pick out the important words in your speech. You are always using the spoken word in conjunction with your signs, which encourages your baby to do the same.

Attention, Please!

Babies learn that they need to have your undivided attention in order to get their message across using signs. As your toddler becomes more active he will want to spend more time away from your ever-watchful gaze as he explores in cupboards and drawers. He doesn't want to have to keep coming back to find you in order to sign for something. He wants to be able to shout his needs to you and have you do all the running, as he is far too busy now!

> As I put 11-month-old Isabella in her car seat she signed that she wanted something to <u>eat</u>. I gave her a biscuit and we set off on our journey. After several minutes of silence Isabella suddenly shouted at the top of her voice, "Mumma, num-nums!" This was the first time she had spoken these words together. My friend informed me that Isabella had been frantically signing <u>more</u> from her seat. Eventually she worked out that she needed to use her voice because I couldn't see her signing to me. — Karyn Warburton

Madeline (12 months old) signs MORE

Frequently Asked Questions

Q. *Why bother teaching baby sign language if my baby will talk eventually anyway?*

1. Baby sign language plays a very important role for your infant when it comes to learning about language, communication and the world around them. It provides a foundation for future language development, knowledge and understanding, and works alongside what a baby finds most natural — using their senses and physical movements in order to learn. The repetition involved with reproducing a sign helps to create and reinforce connections within the brain. Once these pathways have become strengthened sufficiently, they become permanent.

2. Studies have shown that using sign language accelerates learning because babies are able to express their needs and interests at a much earlier stage. Signing babies can practice using language long before they are able to produce the necessary spoken words.

3. Research has also shown that children taught to sign as infants continued to benefit from the experience in later life — scoring higher on intelligence tests and having larger vocabularies than their nonsigning counterparts.

4. A baby is able to understand so much more than we give them credit for, so it makes sense to teach them a way of communicating before they can talk. Babies have so much they want to say and using signs gives them the opportunity. Just think what you and your child could be missing out on!

5. Above all, signing is fun and a great bonding experience for both parent and child. When you teach your baby to sign you are giving them a love of learning that will last a lifetime.

Q. *Will teaching baby sign language delay my baby's speech?*

On the contrary. Studies have shown the opposite to be true. You are never using the sign on its own; it is ALWAYS accompanied by the spoken word. This in turn encourages your baby to try and say the word in conjunction with their sign. For example, your baby may come to you signing ball and saying "ba" simultaneously. Because you keep repeating the word and sign, your baby is given lots of opportunity to hear the word "ball" and will gradually transform "ba" into "ball." At this point, your baby will most likely stop using their sign for ball because they can now say the word perfectly.

Signing actually aids in the acquisition of language as it requires using a physical movement in connection with learning a new word. This helps cement the word, and the concept, in your baby's memory until he has mastered all the skills necessary to produce speech. Making words visual also helps your baby to understand what it is you are talking about.

Q. *Isn't sign language difficult to learn?*

Baby sign language is a collection of easy-to-remember, simplified gestures, based on signs used within the deaf community. Where possible, each sign resembles some characteristic of the object involved, e.g., touching fingertips to lips for <u>eat</u> and patting the top of the head for <u>hat</u>. This makes the signs easy for your baby to learn and easy for you to remember! You are not learning an entire new language, just a core vocabulary of words most popular with babies and parents alike.

Q. *My baby is already saying some words. Is it too late to start teaching signs?*

Research has shown that hearing babies benefit from using signs any time up to 36 months, depending on each child's individual needs. Babies start with a few simple words and it takes a lot of time and effort to build their verbal vocabulary. Some words are more difficult for a child to say — for example, ambulance, helicopter, computer, crocodile or elephant — but this doesn't mean that your toddler isn't interested in these objects or any less keen to talk to you about them. By giving them a sign to use in the interim you are giving them a larger vocabulary to draw on.

Q. *Won't my baby become frustrated when signing to people who don't know sign language?*

Babies tend to use their signs mostly with the people who have been encouraging the signing process. We have kept the signs as iconic as possible, which ensures that they are easily recognized by the majority of nonsigners. Babies are also quick to learn who will respond to their use of signs and who will not. They will attempt to use a sign, and if they get no response they will look for another way to get their point across, either by taking the person to the object they desire or pointing in its direction. Babies are very resourceful!

Q. *Do I have to keep signing once my baby is using a particular sign on a regular basis?*

We recommend that you keep signing as it reinforces to your baby the ongoing importance of communication. However, once your baby is able to say a word in place of a sign, you in turn can stop using the sign. The only exception to this is if you wish to continue with sign language as a second language for your baby.

Chapter 3

Getting Ready
for Signing

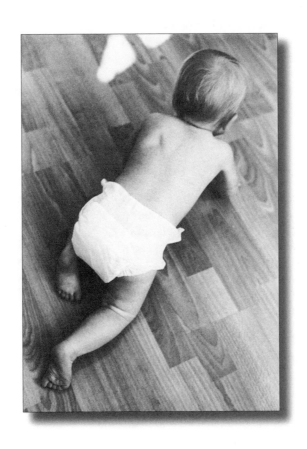

Your Baby's Developing Brain

An infant is born with a brain containing 100 billion neurons that, believe it or not, is only 15 percent complete (the remaining 85 percent will be formed over the next three years). Initially, the majority of neurons are not connected. The main task of your baby's early brain development is to form and reinforce these connections. A baby does this by experiencing life — beginning with forming a close attachment to it's primary caregivers.

Research has shown that what a child experiences during these first few years of life has a direct impact on how their brain will develop, and a baby's early experiences provide a strong foundation for all future learning. This doesn't mean you should be constantly waving flash cards in front of your baby's nose! It is the everyday interactions such as cuddling, feeding, bathing, playing and singing that help a baby to learn at this stage. Loving interactions strongly stimulate a child's brain, which in turn enables synapses to grow, and previously formed connections to become stronger. A baby who receives little stimulation will not develop the same synapses as a child who feels loved, secure and happy, hence their brains will make fewer connections.

Even what may seem to be the most simple of games, like waving good-bye and playing peek-a-boo (which the majority of parents tend to play instinctively), have a great influence on a baby's present and future intellectual, physical and social development.

Presigning Games and Activities

If your baby is too young to begin the signing process (under six months) or is just beginning, there are activities you can try to make it a little easier for him later on.

By giving your infant plenty of opportunities to manipulate objects, explore his environment and participate in games of discovery, he will soon learn:

- 🖐 *How to control and coordinate his movements more precisely, which improves dexterity and strengthens muscle tone.*
- 🖐 *He learns about action-reaction and cause and effect.*
- 🖐 *He learns about making choices and decisions.*
- 🖐 *He learns to solve simple problems for himself.*
- 🖐 *He learns to anticipate an outcome.*
- 🖐 *He is able to understand more about his environment.*

✋ *He learns about taking turns.*

✋ *He becomes more observant.*

✋ *When playing and interacting with you he also learns about the importance of making eye contact.*

These are all necessary skills when learning to sign.

Here are some fun ideas for games that will help your baby with his motor skills, memory, social skills and cognitive development.

Copycat Games

Help with memory, taking turns, concentration, predicting an outcome, coordination and cooperation skills.

Everybody Wave

Try waving to your baby whenever you enter or leave a room. Wave good-bye to Daddy as he goes off to work. Wave at cars as they drive past. Wave good-bye to your baby as you hide behind the sofa and jump out again! Try using a mirror — babies love to look at themselves. Take turns waving to the baby in the mirror. Gently help your baby to wave his own hand if he is having trouble. Once he feels what the movement is like, it will help him to remember the action more easily and can speed up the learning process.

Everybody Clap

Clap your hands during fun activities. For example, build a tower with building blocks and knock it over, then cheer and clap. Your baby will love to watch this activity again and again. Let him have a turn at knocking the tower down. If he is too little to do this then don't be afraid to give him a helping hand.

Clap your hands in time to music or as you sing to your baby. For very small babies you can gently clap their hands together for them as you play.

Touchy Feely

Another fun activity is to pat or point to different parts of your body, naming them as you do so. Touch your head and say, "Mommy's head," then touch your baby's head and say, "Emma's head." Touch your nose, then baby's and continue as long as the activity remains fun and exciting. If your baby is keen, help them to touch their own head, nose or tummy as you say the words. For a slight variation to this theme try kissing your baby on the parts you are naming, making loud kissing noises as you do so. Or for even more enjoyment, try blowing tickly raspberries on your baby's soft skin!

Babbling Babes

Make babbling sounds with your baby. Copy the sounds he makes and repeat them back, for example, "Ba, ba, ba." After a few repetitions, try changing the vowel sound, "Bo, bo, bo." Your infant will be highly amused by this game, and at the same time you are giving your baby a better selection of sounds to draw from. This is a great help as he learns to talk.

Discovery Games

Help with fine- and gross-motor skills, eye-hand coordination, action-reaction, memory, turn-taking, problem-solving and concentration skills.

Look What I Can See!

Very small babies love looking at a wide variety of objects. You can give your infant plenty of visual stimulation by placing a mobile above his bed or by attaching *baby-safe** objects to the side of his cot. Baby gyms are also a great form of amusement for a small baby. They learn to look at, reach out for, touch and eventually grasp the objects swinging tantalizingly above them. Change or alternate these objects every few weeks.

Basket of Discovery

Place a few baby-friendly objects into a basket or cardboard box: rattles, balls, blocks, keys, a small baby-safe mirror, spoons (wooden and metal), basically anything your baby might find interesting. Change the objects once a week to keep your little one busy and interested.

Sorting

Gather a few containers, boxes or pots, some with lids and some without. Using blocks (or items of a similar size) show your baby how to place these objects into the various containers. Place a lid on a container and invite your baby to remove it and find the blocks. Now let him have a turn.

Balls, Balls, Balls!

Collect several balls of varying size and color. Now find a box, something to use as a ramp and a hollow tube. Show your baby how to place the balls into the box and tip them out again. Now try throwing or dropping the balls into the box. Rest one end of your ramp on a coffee table or chair and have the other end in the box. Take turns rolling the balls down the ramp. Now do the same with the tube. If your baby is too little to do this activity on his own he will

---

* The general rule is that if an object can fit into a camera film container, then it is considered a choking hazard for children under three years old.

still enjoy watching what you are doing, and you can keep him entertained for quite a while.

Bonding Games

Games involving lots of cuddles and close contact help your baby to develop a positive sense of self. He learns that he is very important to you and that he is loved. This not only leads to a very strong parent-child bond but helps your baby to build confidence in himself and a strong self-esteem.

Ex-squeeze Me?

Play squeezing games with your baby — they love it! When you give your baby a cuddle, hug him a little tighter than normal and say "Squeeeeeeze!" then release the pressure. Or when you play a chasing game, be a big bear coming to give him a bear hug and follow the same procedure. This may seem like a very simple activity but in fact touch stimulates the brain and is crucial to building a strong relationship with your baby. Expressions of love affect the way your baby's brain forms connections.

May I Have This Dance?

Hold your baby close and dance with him to all kinds of music: children's songs, classical music, rock and roll, and pop music. Your baby will be delighted with this activity.

Sing, Sing a Song!

Don't be afraid to sing out loud to your little one, and don't worry if you are tone deaf, your baby won't care! Sing anything you like, even silly made-up songs, action songs or something from the top 20, because your baby will love them all!

Stories, Please!

Read to your baby. It doesn't matter how little they are, an infant just loves to hear your voice. The whole experience of snuggling up and sharing time together does wonders for you both. After a while you may find your baby will show a preference for a particular story and want to hear it over and over again. This is perfectly normal and helps enormously with memory, comprehension, concentration and listening abilities — all very important prereading skills.

These simple activities can help your toddler develop a love of reading:

- 🖐 *Play with "touch and feel" books.*
- 🖐 *Point to pictures in books and name objects (ideal time to introduce signs!).*

🖐 Reading time becomes an even more stimulating experience for your baby when you bring the stories to life for them. Add a variety of voices for the different characters, pull funny faces, use physical movements and make special-effects-type sounds.

🖐 Point to words as you read. This will draw your toddler's attention to their importance and is a good prereading introduction.

🖐 Try to read daily to your baby, but remember to quit while you're ahead — don't wait until they become bored or upset before you stop. You want these sessions to be fun, so keep it short and leave them wanting more.

Peek-a-boo Games

Every game of peek-a-boo you play with your baby helps give his brain cells a workout by forming and strengthening thousands of connections. Here are some variations to try to keep life interesting:

🖐 Simply cover your eyes with your hands, remove them quickly and say "Boo!"

🖐 Put a towel over your head and repeat the same process as above. Try letting your baby remove the towel for himself. If he is keen, put the cloth over his head and play "Where's the baby gone?"

🖐 Place a toy under a towel or behind a pillow and make it jump out and say "Boo!" Or if your baby is able to move around by himself, let him find the toy. This is a great problem-solving activity.

🖐 Draw a funny face on your thumb, make the face talk or sing to your baby then hide it under your fingers or behind your back. Ask your baby "Where did he go?" Make him reappear again and act very excited saying "Here he is!"

Seb signs BISCUIT

How to Tell When Your Baby Is Ready

Babies will show interest in wanting to take part in the communication process at different stages. Some babies are very alert and interested early on (around six months) and others aren't overly bothered until much later (10 months and beyond), so you need to be observant. Look for the following clues:

And Then I Said…

You may notice your infant watching your face intently when you speak to him and he may even begin silently shadowing the movements your mouth is making as he does so. You might also have one of those babies who enjoy telling great long stories in their own baby language.

Hey! Look at Me!

When you are out you may notice your baby trying to turn his head in all directions at once in order to see what is going on around him. Babies can be very difficult to hold on to at this stage! They become fascinated with their surroundings and other people and will want to interact more. Infants are very adept at getting the attention they feel they deserve. Watch your baby smile cheekily at other people when you are out — he may even attempt to grab hold of them as they try to pass, or squeal as if to say, "Hey, look at me, I'm over here!" if no one has noticed him.

What's That?

Your baby will begin to request names for objects. Depending on the age and physical ability of your baby this can happen a few different ways. A baby, not yet able to crawl, may look at an object, then at you, and back at the object again — as if to say, "What's that?"

When your baby learns to point this becomes a very useful tool for him, not to mention a great game! He will point at everything interesting that catches his eye, wanting to know what it is. The more mobile baby may begin to bring objects to you in order to be told what it is.

These are ideal opportunities to introduce the corresponding sign.

Read Me a Story!

Your baby may begin taking a more active role in your story times and like to point at interesting pictures and be told what they are. Books suddenly become a fascinating object for him as he sits snuggled up next to you learning about his world in a fun, relaxed manner.

Look, I'm Already Doing It!

Can your little one wave good-bye or clap hands? Is he mimicking any other gestures you have shown him? If the answer is yes, then you are already well on your way!

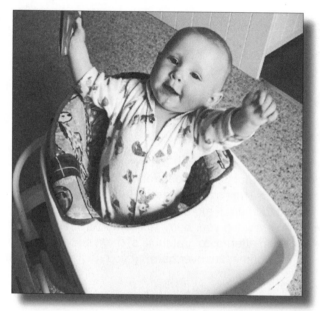

Isabella (7 months old) asking to be picked using an early self-created sign. Almost all babies use this same gesture.

Chapter 4

Getting Started

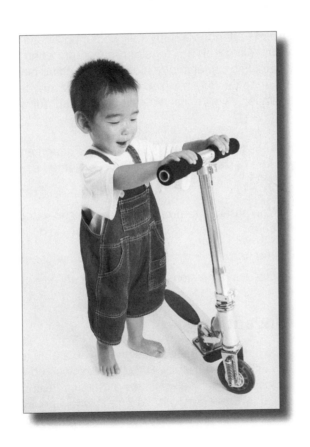

First Signs — Where Do I Begin?

Keep a Record

Before you start, sit down with a piece of paper and write down any signs or gestures you are already using with your baby. Some parents are amazed at this point when they see just how many nonverbal gestures their family has already worked out together without even realizing it! Does your baby raise his arms to be picked up? Blow kisses? Nod his head for "yes" or shake his head for "no"? Or does he rub his eyes when the is tired? How about waving his hands frantically or turning his head from side to side when he has had enough to eat or doesn't like his food?

We had one parent who attended a Baby Talk workshop whose four-and-a-half-month-old baby would smack his lips together repeatedly when he wanted feeding. His mother recognized this signal and responded by feeding him. It wasn't until she was at the workshop that she realized just what a clever young man she had. She would just automatically give him what he had "asked" for without giving it a second thought!

One of our signing dads told us about his 9-month-old daughter who would open and close her hand in a beckoning motion when she wanted something handed to her.

In both these cases the parent interpreted the gesture and responded accordingly. This reinforces the behavior, and encourages your infant to do it again to achieve the same result.

Remember to continue using the signs you and your baby are already using — don't change them, as this will only cause confusion.

Baby's Own Inventions

Babies are very good at creating their own signs. If you are unsure whether your baby is doing this, watch them carefully. Only through close observation will they show themselves. Does your baby always use a certain movement in conjunction with an object or activity? Eleven-month-old Emma would pound her chest with her fists when she wanted something given to her. When 12-month-old Isabella wanted her dancing music on she would point at the stereo and wiggle her diaper-clad bottom.

Megan (11 months old) loved the moon and stars and enjoyed telling people about them. She didn't have the words in order to do this, so instead she created a sign for each object. To talk about the moon she would hold her arm above her head and rotate her hand as if screwing in a lightbulb. She would then go on to "tell" you about the stars by borrowing a movement she had used when performing the action song "Twinkle, Twinkle, Little Star" — both arms up, fingers wiggling. Around the same age Megan also made up a sign for <u>tree</u>. For this movement she held her arm up in front of her. Megan's forearm was the tree trunk and her swaying hand was the branches and leaves.

Megan's twin sister, Louise, was not to be outdone when she made up her sign for <u>spider</u>. Louise adored spiders and would watch and "play" with them for hours. The sign she created involved rubbing the fingertips of her thumb and forefinger together in a pincer-grip style. This came about because the squashing movement showed exactly what usually happened to any poor unsuspecting spider she had found! You can imagine her Mum's reaction when one day she came in doing her <u>spider</u> sign, closely followed by her sign for <u>eat</u>. You guessed it, spider was on the menu that day — YUK!

These are only some of the many signs that Megan and her sister Louise created over the two-year period I was employed as their nanny. It was fascinating to watch how they would teach each other a new sign and "talk" to each other about different things. If Louise was offered a biscuit she would sign <u>eat</u> and <u>more</u> and offer the second biscuit to her sister (most of the time!).

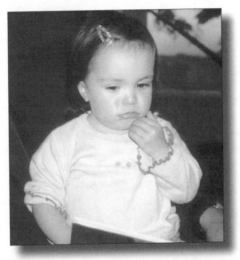

Alyx (16 months old) signs her own made-up version of BIRD. This was created from watching her grandfather whistle using his fingers to create a bird sound

Action Songs and Rhymes

Babies learn action rhymes and songs easily and enjoy this activity immensely. Although they may not yet be able to sing the words, they can still take part by doing the actions along with you. You may notice that it is these actions they begin to borrow when they are making up signs of their own, like Megan did with stars.

How to Teach a Sign

Although we use the word *teach*, all you are really doing is integrating the use of signs into your daily life, to the point that your baby sees them as a natural part of the communication process.

The following list summarizes the key areas you need to remember to ensure that both you and your baby receive maximum benefit from using baby sign language. The list is not intended to be exhaustive, but to remind you of the most important areas.

Key Things to Remember

Sorry, What Were You Saying?

Keep in mind your baby's attention span when introducing signs. The younger the baby the shorter his focus will be. The more fun you make an activity, the longer he will pay attention to what you are doing.

Capitalizing on opportunities for signing in your everyday life is one of the most important points to remember. If you master this, then signing will quickly become a natural activity. Take a moment to think about the daily routines you go through with your baby (e.g., waking, feeding, diaper change, bath time, bedtime). Write down signs that you can use with each of these routines and use them regularly. For example, we used bath time as a great opportunity to teach lots of signs. We decided on our "sign of the day" and would introduce the object and sign as Isabella relaxed in the tub. Firstly, we taught the sign for <u>bath</u>. This is a very simple gesture that most babies around 10 months old can master. Whatever your chosen sign for the day is, make sure you have an example in the bath with them. You may be teaching <u>duck</u>, so have a rubber duck in the bath and play a game with it. Make it kiss your baby's toes or sit on his head. Say "Here comes Mr. <u>Duck</u>" and make the sign simultaneously. "Mr. <u>Duck</u> is going to get your toes!" (Use the sign every time you say the word *duck*. It is also important to make the animal noise, so throw in a couple of good "quack, quacks" as well!) It won't be long before your baby begins asking for the <u>duck</u> game, using the sign you taught him. We used bath time to teach many signs — <u>boat</u>, <u>bubbles</u>, <u>water</u>, <u>frog</u>, <u>fish</u>, <u>swim</u> and even <u>finished/all gone</u> when the bath disappeared down the drain. It was a great help when Isabella was able to tell us when she was <u>finished</u> with her <u>bath</u> — we could get her out before she became tired and restless and, just as importantly, it stopped us trying to get her out *before* she was ready!

Second Nature

Use signs as part of your daily routine. Don't make a "lesson" of it as such; it should be a more natural occurrence. Ideally this is something a baby just gets used to seeing you do when you are talking to and playing with them.

Repeat, Repeat, Repeat, and Then Repeat Some More

Repetition is the key to success. Due to your baby's slowly developing memory, the more often he sees a sign being performed, the easier he will find it to commit them to memory. So your regular input is very important.

 It will feel unnatural at first to keep repeating the sign and the word so often, but keep in mind that this will help your baby to identify the important word in your speech, and associate the sign with it.

I Want to Know What That Is!

Initially, keep signs relevant to your baby's interests. Your baby will show you what he likes best and wants to learn more about. Observe your baby at play to find out what captivates him the most. These will be the objects/ideas he would most likely want to talk to you about, and as a result, these signs will be learned more quickly.

 Be mindful of the times when your baby is tired or hungry, as these are bad times to try to teach signs. Look for teaching opportunities when your baby is exploring, or playing games with you.

Show and Tell

ALWAYS use the sign and word together. Your baby needs to hear spoken language in order to learn how words sound. He will then commit these sounds to memory for future use. Studies have shown that the use of spoken words and signs together makes it easier for your baby to absorb and understand new concepts.

Using the sign and word together is probably the most important point of all. Make sure that your family and other caregivers are aware of this.

Oh, I See What You Mean!

When teaching a new sign, ensure you do so in context. For example, if you are teaching the sign for <u>cat</u>, make sure there is a cat close by that your baby can see. It can be a real cat, toy cat or a picture of a cat, it doesn't matter which — but in order for your baby to understand what you are talking about he needs a physical object to associate the sign and word with.

Look Into My Eyes!

Try to maintain eye contact when showing a new sign to your baby. This can be very difficult when he becomes more mobile, as more often than not he'll be running in the opposite direction! When your baby is requesting a label for a new object he will make eye contact with you. This may be a very brief window of opportunity, so do your best to perform the new sign clearly and repeat both the sign and word several times if possible. Once you know your baby is interested in a particular object, you should try to incorporate the new sign often throughout the day.

Be prepared to make up signs on the spot. Your baby may find something fascinating and immediately look to you for a sign. Don't be afraid to create a sign right there and then, because if you don't, you will miss a great opportunity. Note down your new sign, and make sure your partner and other caregivers use it also. We found that when Isabella was excited about a new object, she picked up the associated sign really quickly, purely because she was interested and was demanding to learn more about it. Try to make your created signs as iconic as possible — almost as if you are trying to mime what the object is. The more your new gesture resembles a particular feature of the subject in question, the easier it will be for you to remember and your baby to relate to.

Variety Is the Spice of Life!

Use a range of items when teaching a new sign. For example, when teaching the sign for <u>fish</u>, use it with real fish, pictures of fish, toy fish, big fish, small fish, fish of all shapes and colors, and even songs about fish. This way your baby is able to build his concept of fish to include several different forms. This is a great way to boost cognitive skills as well.

> I was introducing the sign <u>cow</u> to my 14-month-old using a photograph in a book. We also had a toy cow and we would play a little game to make the activity really fun. One morning we went to a children's farm with some friends and came across some friendly cows. I thought it would be a great opportunity to reinforce the sign we had been working with. I pointed to the cow and did the sign, saying "Look Sam, it's a <u>cow</u> — moooo!" Sam looked at the cow and shook his head. "No!" he replied. It wasn't until the cow actually said "mooo" that he believed me! Looking back I worked out why this was — all the cows we had seen to date had been Friesians (the black and white ones) and the cow at the farm was completely black. Sam must have learned that all cows should be black and white. — Sandra, Christchurch, New Zealand

 Be sure to include lots of sound effects when teaching signs, e.g., use animal noises with animals signs or *vroom* noises when teaching the sign for <u>car</u>. This will help to make the learning process even more exciting.

It's a Family Affair

If possible get the whole family involved. The more people your baby sees using signs the more he will want to take part. Try signing to other members of your family when your baby is watching and he will soon come to realize that these gestures are an important tool for communicating with you. Older brothers and sisters make especially good teachers, and encouraging them to use signs with your baby can also help in the bonding process between siblings. This is especially important when an older child is finding it difficult to accept the new arrival. By giving them a job to do like teaching signs, they feel more involved and love having such an important role to play in their new baby's life.

> My niece Holly, at the age of three and a half, took it upon herself to teach her new sister, Emma, a few signs. Holly proceeded to learn eight of the signs she liked best. She then sat several times a day with her sister and showed her the signs. Emma, of course, showed great interest in what her big sister was doing and the two of them spent many happy moments together. — Karyn Warburton

Bend Me, Shape Me!

Some babies find it helpful if you gently form their hands into the shape required for a particular sign. Once they have experienced how the movement feels it makes it easier for them to remember the sign.

There are a lot of babies out there, however, who do not want this kind of help (my own child included!), so do not persist if they pull their hands away.

> Fifteen-month-old Garth was trying to tell me about a cow he had seen on a poster but couldn't quite manage the sign. Instead of placing his index fingers on the top of his head (as if they were horns), he had them touching his chin. At the same time he made the sign he also said "Mooo!", so I knew exactly what he was talking about. I showed him the sign again and said, "That's right Garth, there is a cow in the picture." He looked at me as I did the sign and tried again but this time he placed his index fingers on his eyes. Realizing he had it wrong but still obviously keen to perfect this sign, I asked him if he wanted me to show him. He nodded enthusiastically and I gently took his hands and placed them on top of his head, with his index fingers pointing up. He was so pleased with himself and from that day on always remembered how to do the sign. — Ulrike, Rotorua, New Zealand

Fun and Games

The more fun you make learning new signs the more involved your baby will become. Even the most simple daily tasks or outings can be turned into wonderful signing adventures. Please refer to the chapter on fun and games for some entertaining songs and activities.

R-E-L-A-X

Don't worry if you forget to sign for a day. Just do them when you remember. At first you may find it difficult remembering to use the signs as often as you would like, but it will soon become second nature. It takes a week or two to really get into the flow. Keep in mind that signing is supposed to be an enjoyable experience for all concerned.

Slowly Does It

Only introduce two or three signs at first. This will make it easier for both yourself and your baby. Easy for you because you are more likely to perform the signs if you only have a couple to think about. Easy for your baby because he is seeing a set number of signs more often, and he needs to see the signs many times before he commits them to memory. Your infant needs time to understand what it is you are showing him, and limiting the number of signs you start with helps him to understand what signing is all about. Some parents find it easier to begin with just one sign. In this case we suggest you start with the sign for milk, but it is really up to you and your personal preference.

Don't Give Up!

Patience truly is a virtue when it comes to signing with your baby. All your efforts will be rewarded eventually. It is up to you to keep the momentum going and don't lose your enthusiasm! You will be so glad you persevered when you see your baby sign their first word.

You may find, as we did, that a lot of the early signs we taught were not repeated back to us initially but could pop up weeks or even months later. We gave up teaching the sign for dummy/pacifier to Isabella after a couple of months because she didn't seem interested in signing it back, and she always had one nearby so didn't need to sign for it. We were amazed when about six months later Isabella used the sign when trying to communicate with her father. She was trying to say the word "dummy" but it just came out as "dee." Giles didn't understand her, so after a few attempts at saying it she used the sign, very clearly and precisely, as if to say, "I said *dummy*, silly!"

I attended a Baby Talk workshop six months ago with my wee one, Liam. I started off with lots of enthusiasm and lots of signs, then remembered I should go slowly and unfortunately my enthusiasm waned. It felt natural to sign and speak as I had done with a deaf girl I lived with once. However, I carried on with a few, milk in particular, then suddenly when I had given up hope he did one back to me! I know this is a story you get frequently and I am sure you know that suddenly my enthusiasm is back. He now picks up signs very quickly — help is the latest one. The cutest is where. It's wonderful to be able to communicate with him in this way and to have a happy toddler (he is 14 months old now) instead of a frustrated one. — Anita, Wellington, New Zealand

Simple Is Best

When introducing your first few signs to your baby, ensure you only use one sign to a sentence. The idea behind baby sign language is that you are only highlighting the important words in your speech — not the entire sentence. For a beginner you need your baby to be able to focus on just ONE movement at a time. Once your baby can happily use two or three signs for himself, it is a good idea to try combining two signs, such as more books, more please, bath finished. This is how your baby will learn to construct his own mini-sentences and build from there.

We often get asked in our workshops how many signs to teach in one go. Avoid the temptation to try to cram in as many signs as possible early on. Initially it makes it easier for you to remember to use your chosen signs when you limit the number of them. You need to use these signs with your baby regularly — if you are trying to work with too many at once your baby may not receive the necessary repetition they require to help them remember the signs.

Everybody Do It — Just Like Me

Make sure that you are consistent and always perform your chosen signs in exactly the same way, regardless of how your baby chooses to do them. You need to praise any and all attempts your baby makes as this will motivate him to keep trying. If your child's fledgling signing efforts are not quite the same as you have shown him, simply repeat the sign back to him in the correct manner (as you would with speech) and say, "That's right, <u>milk</u>. Aren't you clever!" Never say, "No, sweetie, that's wrong, do it like this." Positive reinforcement is strongly recommended — your baby will learn better through encouragement and from copying you. The more practice your baby gets the more proficient they will become. At the end of the day, so long as you understand what your baby is telling you, that's all that matters — after all, that is the ultimate goal of baby sign language!

If other people in your family are using signs as well, ensure you all use exactly the same signs — no one should have their own variation.

Ensure that all other caregivers are consistent with their signs also. We recommend that parents encourage their childcare providers to familiarize themselves with your baby's frequently used signs.

Who's a Clever Baby!

Praise, praise, praise — this is something most parents do naturally anyway. Just make sure that you follow any of your baby's attempts at signing with plenty of enthusiasm. Seeing how pleased and excited you are is reward enough for your baby. We would clap and cheer for Isabella, which she loved. She enjoyed the whole experience so much she began clapping and cheering for herself every time she performed a sign!

Adam signs MOUSE

Starter Signs

For very young babies (six to nine months), we suggest you use the following three beginner signs:

MORE, EAT and MILK. The reason is that these are three things your baby wants and needs often throughout the day. Being a major part of your daily routine, it also makes it easier for you to remember to use the signs during these activities. These beginner signs are easy for your baby to perform as they require the use of large motor skills and are simple movements requiring little coordination. The three signs are also completely different from each other so they will not confuse your baby.

Milk

When teaching the sign for milk say to your baby, "Would you like some milk?" and "Mommy has got some lovely milk for you." When feeding your baby keep talking to him and use your sign whenever you say the word milk. "Is that nice milk?" and "Drink up all your milk." The sign for milk can be used whether you are breast-feeding or bottle-feeding. If you are combining both methods, it may be worth using a different sign for breast-feeding allowing your baby to differentiate between the two. Please refer to the signing dictionary for the breast-feed sign.

I heard a wonderful story about a young mom who had just finished weaning her 15-month-old off breast milk because she was expecting another baby. The toddler was not too impressed about the situation but seemed to accept her mother's reluctant decision. After a hard morning at daycare the now 16-month-old thought she would try her luck and signed to her mother that she wanted to breast-feed (patting the right side of her chest with her right hand). Her mother responded by saying, "Sorry, sweetheart, but there is no more milk," and made the sign for finished/all gone. Not one to give up easily, the little girl then used her left hand to sign on the other side of her chest as if to ask "What about the other side, is there any left in there?" — Karyn Warburton

Eat

Introducing the sign for eat follows exactly the same rules as for milk. This sign covers both words eat and food. "Would you like something to eat?" Offer your baby some food. "Is that nice? Would you like more to eat?" and so on, remembering to sign each time you say the word eat. Sign eat every time you offer food to your baby, whether at mealtimes or "on the run." Also use this sign when you see other people or animals eating, because toddlers are particularly eager to observe other creatures enjoying a snack. Pretend to feed their favorite teddy or use a hand puppet as this adds a whole new exciting dimension to their learning.

More

This may seem like a very abstract sign to begin with, but trust me, it is one babies learn to understand and use quite early on. For some babies (particularly the hungrier ones), "more" is their first word. Introduce this sign when you are doing something fun with your baby. If you are playing a tickling or chasing game, stop before your baby is ready then sign <u>more</u> and ask "Would you like to play some <u>more</u>?" Do the same with other enjoyable activities such as reading time. When you finish a book ask your baby if he would like to hear <u>more</u> stories. Use this sign for anything your baby could possibly want <u>more</u> of (including food) and he will quickly catch on to the idea.

Some additional easy signs include: <u>Up</u>, <u>finished/all gone</u>, <u>hat</u>, <u>where</u>, <u>bath</u>, <u>dog</u>, <u>cat</u>, <u>bird</u>, <u>shoes</u>, <u>help</u>, <u>sleep</u>, <u>telephone</u>, <u>book</u>, <u>ball</u>, <u>swing</u> and <u>light</u>. Look for signs that require large movements, as these will be the easiest options for the younger baby (9 to 12 months).

What Will My Baby's First Signs Look Like?

Your baby's very early attempts at signing can be difficult to recognize initially, so watch closely.

Seb

MILK

When signing <u>milk</u> for the first time your baby will probably use both hands at once. He may hold his hand out in front of his body as you have shown him or, more often than not, his arms will remain down by his sides, hands opening and closing in unison.

Isabella

EAT

The sign <u>eat</u> may appear as a finger pointing into an open mouth or an open hand patting a closed mouth.

Oscar

Jack

Isabella

MORE

<u>More</u> can look as though your baby is attempting to clap his hands together at first or he may bang two closed fists together. Some babies may point an index finger at the other open palm.

In all of these cases praise your baby's attempts and sign back to him the correct way, saying the word as you do so. "Oh, you want some <u>milk</u>? What a clever boy you are! Daddy will get you some <u>milk</u>." This way your infant knows you have understood him, he gets to see the sign performed correctly and he hears how the word is spoken again. As your baby matures, so will his signs, until they more closely resemble what you have shown him.

It is very fortunate for us that babies almost always use their signs when the object they desire is somewhere close by. You can usually work out what sign they are using by having a little look around. If this fails, ask them to point to the object they are talking about, or offer a few possible objects until you discover the right one. It is through this early trial-and-error stage that you work out the meaning of your baby's fledgling signs. Once you know what a sign means you will never look back.

Be aware that all babies have their own signing style, as in the case of 15-month-old Jorge who adopted a form of "signing shorthand," using only one hand to perform some signs such as <u>cow</u>.

When 10-month-old Kassidy was shown the sign for <u>dog</u> (patting your thigh) for the first time she was in her high chair and was unable to pat her own leg. So it transpired that whenever Kassidy saw a dog she would sign <u>dog</u> by patting her mothers thigh and saying "Woof, woof!"

Isabella (13 months old) signs WHERE with one hand because her other is full.

Signs for Older Babies (10+ months)

For older babies it is best to introduce signs for objects they are most interested in; this way you will be sure to succeed. Pets are a great place to start and are a guaranteed winner. Even if you don't have any pets, animals in general are a fascinating subject for your baby. Other signs that may be of great interest are those for transport: car, airplane, train, helicopter, bus, boat and motorbike. They may have a favorite toy: teddy bear, doll, ball or a book. These are all nice easy signs so young toddlers have no trouble learning and using them.

You do not need to teach signs for words your baby can already say. Move on to another word that he hasn't yet mastered and this will give him a larger vocabulary to draw from.

How Long Does It Take?

Many factors influence how long your baby will take to sign back to you:

Your Baby's Age Plays the Biggest Role

Babies under the age of 9 months are still learning how to control their movements. Their coordination skills and memories are limited compared to a baby of 10 or 11 months, who has had a lot more experience and practice.

How and When You Teach a Sign Makes a Big Difference as Well

If you are incorporating signs during a fun activity like story time or playing games, the signs will be picked up more quickly because your infant is kept interested. The signs you use as part of your daily routine will become the norm for him as well.

Some days your baby may not be interested in learning any new signs. He may be tired or unwell or have more important things on his mind — like working out how to get the lid off the cookie jar! On these days it is best just to let him get on with his own agenda. Make sure you keep using your signs, though.

Let Your Baby Choose Signs He Wants to Learn

Observe your baby at play and make a note of what appeals to him most — these will be objects he would most want to "talk" to you about, and it is likely that these signs will be picked up more quickly than others.

With Isabella we found the sign for <u>candy/lollipop</u> was adopted instantly at the age of 10 months. It was obviously something she liked and wanted (as often as she could get it!), and for an entire week it was as though her index finger was glued to the side of her cheek as she signed <u>candy/lollipop</u> frantically!

Other signs like <u>gentle</u> took nearly two months, and <u>pacifier</u> didn't appear until six months later. Your baby will decide where and when he will use his signs and not before.

The more mobile baby will bring items of interest to you in order to learn their names. These "free-range" toddlers have many more opportunities to learn than a baby who is placed in a play pen with the same old toys. Toddlers are generally far more interested in real-life items than most toys anyway. Your baby bringing you one of the treasures they have discovered provides an excellent opening to introduce a new sign and word. These opportunities are ideal, as the lesson was initiated by your baby. You will have his undivided attention!

Give Your Baby the Chance to Use His or Her Signs

Ensure your infant has the opportunity to ask for what he or she wants.

We couldn't understand why Isabella wasn't using the sign for <u>milk</u>, even after six weeks of teaching it. She already used the signs for <u>where</u>, <u>more</u>, <u>book</u> and <u>light</u>, so we knew she understood what we were doing. However, when we sat back and thought about it, we realized that she never needed to ask for her milk, because one of us was always there with a bottle. Our routine was so set that she knew a bottle was on the way. I tested this theory by putting Isabella's bottle on a low table at feed time, making sure Isabella had seen me — but not saying a word. After a few minutes, she realized that I wasn't going to automatically give the bottle to her, so she signed <u>milk</u> and pointed to her bottle! We're not suggesting you hold back on giving things to your baby, but if you find that signs are not being repeated back to you after weeks of trying, then stand back and think about the sign from your baby's perspective. Does he have a need to use the sign, and are you giving him the chance? — Karyn Warburton

Be Prepared for Your Baby to Take a Signing Break

When a baby is learning to crawl or walk this will take up all of his energy and concentration and, for a while, even if he is a champion signer, he will take a break until he has mastered his new skill. Even teething can stop a baby from signing for a while. Once he is ready, the signing will take off again. Keep using your signs though, we don't want you to forget to use them!

 Don't be embarrassed about signing in public. Your baby won't care where you do the signs. Before long, you won't even notice that you are doing them.

An Approximate Timetable

All babies learn at their own pace, but to give you a rough idea of how long it will take before your baby will begin signing back to you, we have created the table below. Some babies are capable of understanding the concept more quickly than our timetable estimates, but most need more time.

4 to 6 months	You can start signing at any stage with your baby, but keep in mind that a very young baby, in most cases, will take many months before they will use signs themselves. This is not to say that they won't begin to recognize the signs' meaning. If you begin signing with your 6-month-old baby you can generally expect to start seeing some results by the age of 9 to 10 months — if you follow our guidelines.
7 to 8 months	A baby's memory skills are expanding daily, and by repeating your signs regularly you are helping with this development. You can expect your baby to repeat a beginner sign in around 8 to 10 weeks on average.
9 to 10 months	A baby's coordination skills are now vastly improved and they will find it easier to perform the more simple signs — e.g., milk, eat, more, finished, bath, help, telephone, light, fish, dog, sleep, hat and shoes. If your baby is showing interest in signing it should only take around four to six weeks on average.
11+ months	A baby is very capable of understanding the whole process in a much shorter time now. By introducing signs for objects that your baby loves you are ensuring a guaranteed result — some signs may be adopted instantly but others may take two to four weeks. Parents and toddlers benefit most from signing between the ages of 12 to 24 months, when frustration, due to otherwise limited communication skills, is at its peak.

 Overall, what you get out of baby sign language is determined by the effort you put in to learning with your baby. Make the learning experience as fun as possible and make use of everyday objects and environments.

How to Recognize the Early Signs of Progress

If you have been signing with your baby for a number of weeks and he still hasn't used any of the signs himself, then here are some ways to check that what you are doing is being absorbed.

Your Baby Pays Closer Attention to Your Hands

Watch your baby when he requests a name for a new object. Once you have been using a few signs for a while you may notice that your baby will begin watching your hands as if waiting to be shown a new sign. Make use of this prompt from your baby to show him new signs while he is in a receptive mood.

Watch to See if Your Baby Attempts to Mimic You

You may notice when you are showing a sign to your baby that he may instantly try to copy the movement. This is a good opportunity to help by gently molding his hands into the correct shape. Only do this if he is keen — never persist if he pulls his hands away.

Be Observant

Remember that your baby's first efforts at signing can look completely different than what you have shown them. You need to be observant. When Isabella first started to sign <u>more,</u> she did so by clapping her hands together and eventually, as her co-ordination matured, she altered her sign to more closely resemble the version that we had been using. It was the same when she attempted to say the word "more." At first it came out as "moh," and after several weeks her new word became a very clear (and loud) "more!"

Please Note: Most babies under nine months of age are unlikely to have the ability to repeat a sign back to you.

An easy way to find out if your baby understands the connection between the signs you have been teaching and the objects they relate to is to play a game. Let's say you have been teaching the sign for <u>book</u> for several weeks and your baby hasn't yet signed it back to you. Sit with a book nearby, where your child can easily find it. Next, ensure your baby is watching you and make the sign for <u>book</u> without saying the word. If he looks toward the book or points and retrieves it, you know he understands the sign. As with spoken words, your baby will recognize the word before he is able to say it himself — he will understand the sign in the same way.

Dos and Don'ts

This section summarizes the key points to remember when introducing signs to your baby, and also the negative actions to avoid. Be sure to use common sense when starting out, and let your baby set the pace that he is comfortable learning at. Try and get the support of your family and friends to help to teach the signs to your baby. The more people your baby has signing with them, the more quickly he will pick up new signs and the more people he will have to "talk" to.

Dos

- Start slowly — *no more than three signs at first.*
- Use signs as part of your daily routine.
- Repeat, repeat, repeat and then repeat some more.
- Relevance — *teach signs of interest to your baby.*
- Be consistent — *always sign the same way.*
- Be patient — *allow plenty of time for your baby to catch on to the idea.*
- Be observant — *watch for opportunities to introduce new signs.*
- **ALWAYS** *say the word when showing a sign.*
- Keep it simple — *sign one word per sentence at first.*
- Be enthusiastic — *encourage and* **PRAISE!**

Don'ts

- **NEVER** *pressure your baby into signing.*
- **NEVER** *withhold something until your baby signs for it.*
- **DON'T** *correct your baby's signing attempts.*
- **DON'T** *expect your baby to sign on demand.*
- **AVOID** *showing disappointment.*

Chapter 5

The Advanced Signer

Moving on from Beginner Signs

Select Signs for Objects Your Baby Is Interested in

Once your baby understands one or two of the beginner signs try adding a couple more fun ones (the easier signs for animals, toys or transport are ideal). When your child has used two or three signs on his own you can begin to sign for as many things as you like — your baby will choose the signs he likes best and will use them accordingly.

Combining Signs

Now that your baby has a few signs in his vocabulary it is a good time to begin combining signs to create simple sentences, for example, <u>more milk</u>, <u>more books</u>, <u>where's teddy?</u> By watching you creating basic sentences he too will soon learn how to do it on his own. Your baby's first sentence may be a combination of signs or words and signs together. Try choosing some signs that will be helpful for you as well as your baby. Signing parents and caregivers have found the following signs very useful.

Hot

It was extremely important for me to teach this sign to the babies I worked with, particularly the early walkers, as they were able to gain access to dangerous objects much more easily. I thought this might be a difficult concept for a baby (around 11 or 12 months) to grasp, but was pleasantly surprised to find it one of the easiest. In order to teach about temperature you need to allow your infant to safely feel what you are talking about. Baby Talk parents came up with a few very good techniques to help with this. One parent allowed her child to place her hand on a recently emptied coffee cup that was still quite warm. Another filled a hot water bottle with hot tap water for her child to feel. The best way we found was by standing a safe distance away from our fireplace (at least eight feet), where you can still feel the intense heat coming from the flames. I would point at the fire, say "hot," and perform the sign at the same time, repeating both word and sign several times. We then moved on to the oven, heater and heated towel rail, each time repeating the process.

Please Note: Although your signing baby learns to understand the meaning of HOT, you still need to ensure that all hot objects are safely out of their reach or have a protective barrier around them.

It only took a few days before Isabella (12 months old) began using the sign for herself. She would stand well back from the hot object, point and repeat her sign, saying "Hoh." She then began to notice other things that were hot — our cat, for instance had been lounging in the sun all day long and his fur was almost smoldering. Isabella went over to play with him and touched his fur. She instantly came running over to me doing her sign for <u>cat</u> followed closely by her sign for <u>hot</u>. She was very excited! A few weeks later Isabella began using her new sign to tell us when her food, milk or bath was too hot or if the pavement was too hot to walk on in bare feet. About a month later this sign began to evolve even further. Whenever Isabella came across an object she hadn't seen before, she would "ask" us if it was <u>hot</u> before she would touch it. She would point to the object and look back at us with a quizzical look on her face and sign <u>hot</u>?
— Karyn Warburton

Cold

We used a similar tactic when teaching the sign for <u>cold</u>. This involved standing in front of the freezer with the door open and an ice cube in each hand! We also talked about water being cold or when it was cold outside. It was a great help when Isabella could tell us when she felt too <u>cold</u> — this was always a worry for me, especially at bedtime.

Gentle

Another very useful sign to teach if you have pets or a younger baby, or when you just want to show your infant how to be careful with more delicate objects. You will find the concept of being gentle comes across in the way you teach it. For example, when you are patting a tiny kitten and showing your baby how to be gentle, you tend to be crouched down, speaking in a quiet voice, using slow, careful movements as you lovingly stroke its fur — your body language says it all!

Isabella was anything but gentle with our own cat and had several scratches to prove it. We had been trying to teach the <u>gentle</u> sign for her own protection but she seemed to much prefer taunting the poor thing instead. I became especially worried about how she would react when we went to visit my sister's new baby. My concern proved to be unfounded when Isabella walked straight up to her new cousin (with me close behind!), made her sign for <u>gentle</u> (which to date she hadn't used), kissed baby Emma on the head and ran off to play with more exciting things. I was dumbfounded to say the least. My first thought was *This is not my child!* It just goes to show how much they do take in and only when the time feels right for them will they use the signs they have stored away. — Karyn Warburton

Pain/Hurt

The concept of pain is surprisingly easy to teach. When your baby is crawling and learning to walk they are hurting themselves frequently. When this happens, give your baby lots of cuddles and comfort, and once the tears have subsided make the pain/hurt sign at the point where the pain is occurring: a bumped head, a sore toe, or a banged knee. Another way to reinforce the sign (which Isabella found highly amusing) is to pretend to hurt yourself. Try accidentally bumping your knee on the coffee table, or better still, have teddy or dolly hurt themselves. On one occasion my husband, Giles, really did hurt himself when getting Isabella out of the bath. Before he had the chance to make the sign for pain/hurt, Isabella was already doing it for him.

> One morning when dressing Isabella to go out she began to make her sign for pain/hurt, and as she did so, said, "Daddy, ouch." She did the sign near her foot, and upon closer inspection I remembered that she had a sore toe. I was amazed that she had used her sign to warn me to be careful when putting her socks on.
> — Giles Warburton

Help

This is one of the best signs for helping your baby become more independent. We found teaching the help sign was more of a necessity for us. Our daughter was a very independent toddler and liked to try things out for herself, and heaven help you if you intervened prematurely! Having taught the sign for help, we just needed to observe and wait until we were asked to lend a hand. Everybody was happy.

In order to teach this sign, watch your child at play. If it looks as though he may need some help, walk over and ask, "Do you want Mommy to help?" — using the sign as you speak. If he gives you any indication that your help is not yet required — either by shaking his head no, squealing or pushing you away, quietly back off again. Wait another few minutes and if your baby is still struggling then try it again. This routine will soon become a habit for you, and your baby will come to realize that all he needs to do is pat his chest and you will come to his aid, and not before.

This is a nice easy gesture that even young babies can use (10 months). It is a wonderful thing to give such a small child the ability to ask for help as and when they need it, and it really boosts their sense of independence.

Diaper Change

We tried teaching this sign, but Isabella wasn't keen, as she loathed having her diaper changed. If I did the <u>diaper change</u> sign in our house it meant run and hide! With the twins Megan and Louise, Louise would always use the sign but Megan wasn't interested.

Maybe this sign would be easier to teach if you are using cloth diapers on your baby, as the disposable diapers available these days are very good, and your baby doesn't experience that awful wet feeling. Babies do know when they have messed themselves, however, regardless of which kind of diaper you are using. This fact is usually blatantly obvious to you also, and a sign is not necessary!

Having said that, I know several daycare centers that have experienced great success with this sign. So, it is definitely worth a try.

Don't Touch/No

An extremely helpful sign. We noticed that we were more likely to be ignored when we used just spoken words alone, and found we were constantly repeating ourselves. Isabella came to realise that when we used the <u>don't touch/no</u> sign, we really meant it. The sound of your hands clapping together, accompanied by the shaking of your head and a nice firm "no!" helps your child understand better.

If you have used the sign and your toddler continues to persevere with the unacceptable activity, repeat the sign and word again. If you are ignored a second time repeat the sign once more then remove him from the situation, distracting him with another, more exciting activity — in another room if necessary. Your baby will soon learn the rules of action and consequence with two warnings, then the action — strike three, you're out! This way he knows what the boundaries are and just how far he can push them.

I knew Isabella understood this sign when I saw her using it with our puppy, who was chewing one of her toys at the time!

Finished/All Gone

Another great sign for helping a toddler as they strive for independence. Introduce this sign at the end of meals, when you have finished playing or at the end of a story. We have heard from many parents how useful this sign has been for them and the different ways a baby will use it. Some infants will sign <u>finished/all gone</u> when somebody leaves the room. Others use the sign to tell you when something is "broken," such as when they have just squashed a bug!

Isabella (then 12 months old) used this sign in a rather amusing way when standing in a supermarket queue. She began to stare at the man in front of us. He was completely bald and his head was extremely shiny. Isabella looked at the man's head then back at me. Frowning she used her sign for <u>hair</u> then followed up with the sign for <u>finished/all gone</u>. It was a struggle to stop from laughing out loud! — Karyn Warburton

Daniel (11 months old) signs FINISHED

I attended a Baby Talk workshop six weeks ago and began teaching my nine-month-old baby, Daniel, the food-related signs. He was just getting going on crawling so our progress had been fairly slow, but we've both been enjoying ourselves. He sometimes signs <u>more</u> and <u>eat</u> and seemed to understand <u>finished/all gone</u> but had never actually signed it as he **loves** his food.

A few weeks ago, when he was 11 months old, I gave him a peanut butter sandwich. I'd given him one for the first time the previous day and he scoffed it down with enthusiasm. On this occasion, however, Daniel held the sandwich and put it to his mouth briefly, then dropped it and began vigorously signing <u>finished/all gone</u>.

Because of this, I immediately knew something was very wrong and looked carefully at his hands and mouth to see a rash and swelling and then a minute or so later he began crying and itching. I rushed Daniel to the doctor and was told he had a peanut allergy that was potentially life-threatening, although in Daniel's case it hadn't affected his breathing. (The allergy often only becomes apparent the second time a child eats something — the first time the reaction is set up in their system.) I'm really glad he could use this sign because, although he obviously knew something was very wrong immediately, I think that if he hadn't done it I would have just assumed he was fussing with his food and tried to coax him into eating it. — Anne Robinson, Wellington, New Zealand

Teaching Good Manners

Many parents, myself included, have had great success with teaching <u>please</u>, <u>thank you</u> and <u>sorry</u>. Politeness is something that can be instilled at a young age.

How you speak to your child will in turn reflect how he will speak to you and other people. If you always say "please" and "thank you" to your baby, it will become a natural part of his own character. Whenever your baby gives something to you, sign and say <u>thank you</u> in return. Try asking your baby to pass you an object using the <u>please</u> sign. If your baby signs for a <u>cookie</u> or <u>milk</u>, gently remind him to sign/say <u>please</u> by signing it yourself each time. Don't withhold an object until your baby signs <u>please</u> or <u>thank you</u>, as this is a very negative thing to do, and will only ensure your infant never uses the sign.

Adam signs PLEASE

Teach <u>sorry</u> whenever your toddler hurts another person or animal. You could then also encourage the concept of <u>gentle</u> by teaching the corresponding sign.

Signs for Feelings

Teaching your child to express how he feels is a wonderful thing to do. If your toddler can tell you when he feels sad, frightened or angry you can take steps to find out why and resolve the situation. Many adults find expressing themselves a difficult task, so starting from a young age can only be a good thing. When teaching signs for <u>happy</u>, <u>sad</u>, <u>cry</u> and <u>angry</u>, try using the song "If You're Happy and You Know It" (see the chapter on fun and games). Use your body language and facial expressions to get the idea across so your child can understand.

Adam signs SAD

Signs for Favorite People

We have found the signs that work best when talking about people such as grandparents or aunts and uncles were ones we created ourselves. Look for a characteristic of that person when making up a sign, i.e., do they wear glasses? Does the person wear a hat often? Does Grandma wear a necklace or cardigan you could make up a sign for? Does Grandpa have a moustache? Some children even talk about "Big Nana" and "Little Nana" by way of differentiating. You may find that your baby can say "Nan" and "Pop" quite early on anyway. This is one reason we never bothered teaching the signs for <u>mother</u> and <u>father</u> — these were Isabella's first words, "Mum Mum" and "Dad Dad."

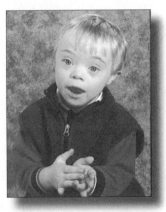

Brendon signs MOMMY

Transition from Signs to Speech

 You may find that your baby chooses to say the word instead of using the sign, which is great! By always using the word and sign together you are giving him the option. In these cases you don't need to keep using the sign, but do still repeat the word so that your baby can perfect his pronunciation.

The transition to speech occurs in three stages:

1. *Your baby will use the sign on its own for a while, or sometimes just the sound that the object makes.*

2. *Your baby will use the sign and attempt to say the word in conjunction with it.*

This is a great help to parents as many first words are difficult to decipher. If your baby uses a sign at the same time, then his attempt at saying the word is instantly understood. This saves a great deal of frustration for both of you, and your baby loses none of his confidence as he attempts to use spoken language.

The success he experiences really boosts his self-esteem and spurs him on to keep talking. When your baby tries out a new word, for example "milk," it may initially come out as "muh." Having recognized what he is trying to say, the best thing a parent can do is to repeat the word correctly back to him: "That's right, 'milk,' well done." This way your baby is able to hear again how the word actually sounds, which will aid him in subsequent attempts. By giving him praise you are also encouraging him not to be afraid to try again.

Never correct your baby's words: "No, not 'muh,' say 'milk.'" Try not to adopt "baby words" either — this can be very difficult as they can come up with some very cute-sounding words! Remember, your little one is relying on you to model real words for them to imitate.

3. *The final step is when the words take over and the signs just drop away.*

This can be a little sad for parents because learning to sign with your baby is such a fun, positive experience for both of you. But your ultimate goal has been reached — one of the aims, after all, is to help your baby talk sooner. At the age of 18 months, we found that although Isabella could say all the words she had signs for, occasionally the signs would still be used. When she was particularly excited about something she would combine signs and words again as if trying to highlight what she was talking about. When she wanted something "right this minute!" she still used her <u>more</u> sign along with the word, but with more emphasis. The other times we saw Isabella using her signs were when she had her mouth full or just wanted to be cute!

 If you are teaching a recognized signing system as a second language and you don't want the signs to disappear, then all you need to do is keep using them yourself and encourage your baby to do the same.

Troubleshooting

Listed below are the most common problems parents and caregivers come up against when signing with their babies and toddlers, and some helpful advice. Remember to keep in mind that all babies learn and develop at different rates and you should avoid comparing your baby to what others the same age are doing.

I have been signing with my baby for quite a while now (he is now 10 months old), and I know he understands the signs I am using because he will respond accordingly — i.e., if I sign <u>milk</u>, he will look at the bottle and grin at me, but doesn't use the sign himself.

This is a very common phase and is perfectly normal. Believe it or not it is also a very good indication that your baby is becoming more aware of what you are doing. Just make sure you are not overwhelming your baby with too many signs to begin with, as initially they need to see FEWER signs, MORE often. Learning to sign is the same as learning to speak. Your baby will first understand the signs shown to him, then the next stage is realizing he can use the signs in order to communicate a need or idea to you. Once your baby uses one or two signs for himself there will be no stopping him.

My baby began to sign at the age of 10 months and was doing really well (she could use 10 signs!), but now she has suddenly stopped altogether. She is learning to walk at the moment; does this have anything to do with it?

You are correct about the walking stage taking precedence over the signing. Your baby needs to put all her energy and efforts into learning to walk, so everything else will be put on hold until she has mastered her new skill. Just keep signing to her as usual and be patient. Your daughter hasn't forgotten her old signs and still understands what you are showing her. Even cutting new teeth can interrupt the signing process for a while.

I was so excited when my 8-month-old baby began to use the sign for <u>milk</u>. At first we thought it was our imagination but she was definitely doing it because even my mother noticed. The only problem we have now is that she is signing <u>milk</u> for everything! Have I confused her in some way? How can I make her understand that this sign is only used when she is "talking" about milk?

No you haven't confused your baby. Again, this is a natural progression and is a developmentally appropriate stage all new signers (and talkers) go through. Your baby has realized that she has communicated something to you by the positive reaction she received when she used the sign. She is now using the sign repeatedly in order to get the same reaction. It is the same when they begin to make their prespeech sounds, like "baba." Their parents show great delight and often mimic the noise back, and excited by this interaction, the baby will repeat the sound. If you are unsure as to whether your daughter is actually asking for milk, try offering some to her and sign <u>milk</u> — if she accepts the milk then you have reinforced the sign for her and she has received what she requested. If she does not want the milk, you have still reinforced the sign and she will begin to associate the sign she is making with the milk appearing. Initially it will take a great deal of patience, perseverance and repetition on your part, but it is well worth the effort. Continue to sign with her in the usual way — if you are only using one sign at the moment try introducing another such as <u>more</u> or <u>eat</u>. This will not only give your baby a larger vocabulary but will help her to work out that different signs stand for different things.

I started using the three beginner signs with my ten-month-old about six weeks ago and he seems to understand the signs but is not using them. He is a fussy eater so I don't expect he would want to "ask" for <u>milk</u> or something to <u>eat</u>. Are there any other signs I could try?

All babies have their own interests and agendas — some are only concerned about where their next meal is coming from and others, like your own baby, are not bothered about feeding times. In this case, think about what really excites your baby, i.e., do you have a pet cat, dog, fish or bird? These are all easy signs to learn and teach. Does your baby enjoy having a bath? Or does he have a fascination with lights? Does he have a teddy, a book, a ball or other toy he really likes? These are all suitable signs to teach a young baby.

Oscar signs EAT

Chapter 6

Fun and Games

Keeping It Fun

It goes without saying that the more fun you make learning signs the more enthusiastic your baby will be. So let your imagination run wild. You don't need to come up with complicated games. Any games that involve chasing, hiding, tickling, lots of noise and laughing are ideal. Use books, songs, games, outings, toys, puppets and animals, and anything else you think your child will enjoy.

Try some of the following activities:

Toddlers love it when you dress a teddy bear in some of their clothes. Put a pair of baby shoes on ted and watch your baby's face light up. You can then teach two signs in one go. "Look at <u>teddy</u>, <u>teddy</u> has got your <u>shoes</u> on!" You could also place your baby's hat on teddy's head and teach a sign for that as well. "Look, now <u>teddy</u> has got your <u>hat</u> on. What a silly <u>teddy</u>!" Then go on to sing to the tune of "The Sun Has Got His Hat On."

<u>Teddy's</u> got your <u>hat</u> on,
Hip, hip, hip, hooray.
<u>Teddy's</u> got your <u>hat</u> on
And he's going out to <u>play.</u>

Good old ted can teach many a sign if you put your mind to it. Here's some more teddy bear examples:

Teddy Bear, Teddy Bear

<u>Teddy bear</u>, <u>teddy bear</u>,
Turn around.
<u>Teddy bear</u>, <u>teddy bear</u>,
Touch the ground.
<u>Teddy bear</u>, <u>teddy bear</u>,
Go <u>up</u> the stairs.
<u>Teddy bear</u>, <u>teddy bear</u>,
Brush your <u>hair</u>.
<u>Teddy bear</u>, <u>teddy bear</u>,
Switch off the <u>light</u>.
<u>Teddy bear</u>, <u>teddy bear</u>,
Say good night. (*Sign <u>sleep</u>*)

One day I was watching 13-month-old Isabella play with her teddy bear. I was completely amazed to observe her teaching him the sign for <u>ball</u>. She found a ball in her toy box and brought it over to Mr. Ted. She showed it to him then placed it on his lap. She then proceeded to teach him the sign and say "ba" at the same time. Isabella then picked up the ball again and showed it to Mr. Ted and repeated her sign. It was then I knew she really understood the signing concept. I just wish I'd had a video camera handy! — Giles Warburton

Try teaching <u>eat</u> using a hand puppet. Sit beside your baby and have an empty bowl and a spoon as props. Say, "Do you think Polly Puppet would like something to <u>eat</u>?" Show them the sign. Then ask the puppet. "Would you like something to <u>eat</u>?" (Repeat the sign.) Have your baby feed the puppet or do it yourself if he doesn't want to. If your baby is keen, place the puppet on his hand. This will give him an opportunity to sign <u>eat</u> on behalf of the puppet. You could also teach <u>drink</u> and <u>milk</u> the same way. The only problem with puppets is that you can only teach the one-handed signs!

More songs and rhymes to help reinforce signs:

Rain

Pitter patter, pitter patter,
The <u>rain</u> goes on for hours,
And though it keeps me in the <u>house</u>,
It's very good for <u>flowers</u>.

All the Bunnies... (*Use the sign for <u>rabbit</u>*)

All the <u>bunnies</u> fast <u>asleep</u>.
All the <u>bunnies</u> not a peep.
If I should <u>sing</u> my song today,
Will all those <u>bunnies</u> come out and <u>play</u>?
(*Children get up and hop around room*)
Hop little <u>bunnies</u> hop, hop, hop,
Hop little <u>bunnies</u> hop, hop, hop.
Hop little <u>bunnies</u> hop, hop, hop,
Hop little <u>bunnies</u> hop and <u>stop</u>!

This song can easily be adapted for any other animal. Try jump little froggies, fly little birdies, or even run little doggies.

Pussycat, Pussycat

<u>Pussycat</u>, <u>pussycat</u>,
<u>Where</u> have you been?
I've been to London to visit the Queen.
<u>Pussycat</u>, <u>pussycat</u>,
What did you do there?
I <u>frightened</u> a little <u>mouse</u> under a chair!

Five Little Ducks

Five little <u>ducks</u> went out to <u>play</u>,
Over the hills, and far away.
Mother <u>duck</u> said "Quack, quack, quack, quack,"
But only four little <u>ducks</u> came back.
(*Continue to count down until there are no little
    ducks, then sing:*)
No little <u>ducks</u> went out to <u>play</u>,
Over the hills and far away.
Mother <u>duck</u> said "Quack, quack, quack, quack,"
And all the little <u>ducks</u> came waddling back.

Five Little Monkeys

Five little <u>monkeys</u> jumping on the <u>bed</u>,
One fell off and <u>hurt</u> his head.
Mummy <u>phoned</u> the <u>doctor</u> and the <u>doctor</u> said
"No more <u>monkeys</u> jumping on the <u>bed</u>!"
(*Sing with 4, 3, 2, 1 little monkeys then . . .*)
No little <u>monkeys</u> jumping on the <u>bed</u>,
None fell off and <u>hurt</u> his head.
Mummy <u>phoned</u> the doctor and the doctor said,
"Put those <u>monkeys</u> back in <u>bed</u>!"

Little Miss Muffet

<u>Little</u> Miss Muffet
<u>Sat</u> on a tuffet,
<u>Eating</u> her curds and whey.
Along came a <u>spider</u>,
Who <u>sat</u> down beside her
And <u>frightened</u> Miss Muffet away.

The Where Song

(*You can change teddy to any other object*)

<u>Where</u> is <u>teddy</u>?
<u>Where</u> is <u>teddy</u>?
Here I am.
Here I am.
How are you today <u>friend</u>?
Very well, <u>thank you</u>.
<u>Hide</u> away.
<u>Hide</u> away.

The Eat or Milk Song

(You can change lyrics to drink your milk)

Eat your dinner.
Eat your dinner.
Please, please, please.
Please, please, please.
Eat it up for Mummy,
Fill up your little tummy. (*pat your stomach*)
Now it's gone, it's all gone.

The More Song

(Sung to the tune of "I'm a Little Teapot")

I'm a hungry baby,
I want more.
More, more, more, please,
Can I have some more?
I'll eat up all my dinner,
Then I'll shout;
"Put me to bed,
I'm all tired out!"

I Want to Go Outside!

I want to go outside,
Please, please, please.
I want to see the flowers
And the little buzzing bees.
I like to watch the airplanes
Flying in the sky
And all the cars,
As they go driving by.
But most of all I just love
To run and jump and shout.
So please, please, please,
Please let me out!

The Shoe Song

(Sung to the tune of "Polly Put the Kettle On")

Come and put your shoes on.
Come and put your shoes on.
Come and put your shoes on.
We're going out to play!

The Goodnight Song

The <u>stars</u> are in the sky
and the <u>moon</u> is shining bright.
Now it's time to go to <u>bed</u>
and turn off the <u>light</u>.
<u>Sssshhhh</u>, good night. (*Use the sign for <u>quiet</u>*)

Animal Sounds

What does the <u>dog</u> say?
Woof, woof, woof.
What does the <u>cat</u> say?
Meow, meow, meow.
What does a <u>bird</u> say?
Tweet, tweet, tweet.
But the little tiny <u>fish</u>
says nothing at all! (*Open and close your mouth like a fish*)

My Pets

I have a <u>mouse</u>,
He lives in my <u>house</u>.
I have a <u>cat</u>,
My <u>cat</u> wears a <u>hat</u>.
I have a <u>dog</u>,
Who's friends with a <u>frog</u>
What do you think about that?

Down on the Farm

(*Sung to the tune of "The Wheels on the Bus"*)

The <u>horse</u> on the farm goes neigh, neigh, neigh,
neigh, neigh, neigh,
neigh, neigh, neigh.
The <u>horse</u> on the farm goes neigh, neigh, neigh,
All day long!

Choose a different animal and repeat the song — try a duck, dog, cow, pig, sheep, chicken, rooster, cat or even a turkey. You can easily change this song to include wild animals — down at the zoo!

Help Me!

<u>Help</u> me, <u>help</u> me,
I <u>hurt</u> my head,
Because I fell right out of <u>bed</u>!

<u>Help</u> me, <u>help</u> me,
I'm in <u>pain</u>.
I think it's those pesky <u>teeth</u> again! (*Point to your teeth*)

<u>Help</u> me, <u>help</u> me,
I <u>hurt</u> my knee.
I banged it on the ground you see. (*Tap the floor*)

I need a <u>hug</u>,
A <u>kiss</u> and a <u>cuddle</u>.
Then I'll do my best
To keep out of trouble!

If You're Happy and You Know It

If you're <u>happy</u> and you know it,
Clap your hands. (*Clap, clap*)
If you're <u>happy</u> and you know it,
Clap your hands. (*Clap, clap*)
If you're <u>happy</u> and you know it
And you really want to show it.
If you're <u>happy</u> and you know it,
Clap your hands. (*Clap, clap*)

For the next verse sing, "If you're <u>sad</u> and you know it,
have a <u>cry</u>." (*Sob, sob!*) And lastly add, "If you're <u>angry</u>
and you know it, stamp your feet." (*Stamp, stamp!*)

In My Car

I'm driving in my <u>car</u>.
I'm driving in my <u>car</u>.
Brmmm, brmmm, toot, toot (*Press your nose for the
    car horn*)
I'm driving in my <u>car</u>!

Hiding Games

1. Sit on the floor with your baby and play this fun hiding game. Have at hand an
   object that your baby loves — a book, ball, doll or teddy. Play with it for a minute
   or two and then hide it under a towel or box. Now use your sign for <u>where</u>. Say
   and sign "<u>Where</u> is the <u>ball</u>?" Your baby will love finding his toy for you and will
   want to play it again and again. This simple and highly entertaining game can be
   used to teach many signs. After the tenth game in a row you can use your sign
   for <u>finished/all gone</u> to end the session!

2. Once your child is familiar with a few signs try this game: Hide a toy animal, for example, under a box and tell him there is something hiding inside (use the sign for <u>hide</u>) — "What can it be?" Then do the sign for the concealed item and see if he can guess what it is. Invite him to have a look. Be very excited when your child discovers the animal and show him the sign again — encouraging him to have a try (don't forget to use the animal sound as well!).

What's in the Bag?

Find a brightly colored bag or pillowcase and place a few objects inside it (ones you want to teach signs for). The bag I use has flowers and bees on it. My daughter loves to look at the bag and I show her the signs for bee and flower before we start our game. Let your baby pull out one object at a time. Be very enthusiastic and ask what he has found. Show him the corresponding sign and sing a little song about the object. For example, if you have a toy spider in your bag, try singing "Little Miss Muffet." If you don't know a song or rhyme just make one up — your baby won't mind at all!

Story Time

Make up simple stories that incorporate the signs you are introducing. Use a storyboard, magnets or toys to make the whole lesson as fun and engaging as possible.

Signing Book

Create a signing book with your child. Place pictures of family members inside and teach the signs for <u>mother</u>, <u>father</u>, <u>baby</u>, <u>sister</u>, <u>brother</u>. Photos of pets are also very good. Think of the signs you wish to teach your child and spend time together searching for pictures of these objects in old magazines. Cut them out and glue these into his sign book as well.

Routines

Make up a simple bedtime routine and follow the same format every night. Babies thrive on having a regular routine as it allows them to anticipate what is going to happen next. A really simple ritual we created helped Isabella learn lots of new signs. Hang a collection of pictures on your baby's wall — animals, vehicles and anything else fun. Start with three and add a new one each week. Every evening say goodnight to each picture using the sign, word and sound (if it makes one). This will help your baby become familiar with these new signs quite quickly.

Chapter 7

Signing Experiences

Signing in a Childcare Center

With Ulrike Gaul

Not all children are able to learn using traditional teaching methods, and as a result they fall behind in class. These children need to be able to experience learning on a more physical level, and signing is a great way to facilitate this approach to learning. No child should ever miss out on their education because of their different learning style. Many daycare centers and junior classes now incorporate a certain amount of sign language into their curriculum.

Ulrike Gaul, an early childhood educator and supervisor in the under-twos section at Alpha Childcare Centre in Rotorua, New Zealand, began introducing the Baby Talk signing system in September 2002 with great success. Ulrike and staff began to gradually integrate the signs into their daily routines. Here's how.

"With the younger babies (under nine months) we started with the sign for <u>milk</u>, which was shown to them during feed times. One eight-month-old baby loved to see me using the sign <u>milk</u> while she was having her bottle. She would grin at me and closely watch what I was doing. After a few days she began to place her hand in mine each time I used the sign, as if she wanted to feel how it was done. A week later she placed her little hand in mine, as was now our routine, only this time she pulled her hand out again and performed the sign for herself. She could see how thrilled I was and continued to sign away frantically at me — she was just as excited!"

Garth signs HORSE

Staff decided that for the older babies (10 months and above) it would be best to introduce a few of the more exciting signs during mat time, singing and play times.

The idea was that once the children picked up and used a few of the more fun signs and understood the process of communicating with their hands, the subsequent learning of more abstract signs would be less difficult.

"Using the all-time favorite 'Old MacDonald Had a Farm,' the teachers included signs for <u>cat</u>, <u>dog</u>, <u>horse</u>, <u>cow</u>, <u>pig</u> and <u>chicken</u>. It was so entertaining to watch as all the children, including most of the younger ones who couldn't yet walk or sing, became very animated using signs and animal sounds. The more signs we introduced using songs, stories, pictures and games,

Adam signs WHERE

the more they wanted to learn. Because the majority of signs we use are iconic, they give meaning to words and make it easier for babies to understand what you are talking about.

"One young boy in my group was born eight weeks premature, so naturally his development was slower than others the same age. Using baby sign language just seemed to fit with his way of learning and understanding. He was 20 months old when we introduced the Baby Talk system and within two months he had learned over 100 signs. I was struggling to keep up with him! His spoken language, which was limited previously, began to take off as well."

What Next?

Once the children began to use a few of the fun signs, teachers started to introduce other important signs, particularly those that help with independence, discussing feelings and teaching good manners.

Garth signs WORK

"We used the signs for <u>please</u> and <u>thank you</u> throughout the day as we interacted with each child and at meal times. Three more great meal-time signs were, <u>finished/all gone</u>, <u>more</u> and <u>help</u>. I remember on one occasion when we had jelly for desert, the children did their best to feed themselves, but within minutes all began to use the <u>help</u> sign. Until this stage most of them hadn't used this sign. We were very excited (not to mention amused) at this breakthrough!

"I also wanted to teach about turn-taking so began to introduce the sign for <u>wait</u>. An ideal opportunity to use this sign arose when I noticed children pushing each other on the slide. I stood at the top of the slide and as each child climbed the stairs to have their turn I would sign <u>wait</u> until the previous child was completely clear. The children soon got the idea for themselves, only requiring my intervention on the odd occasion.

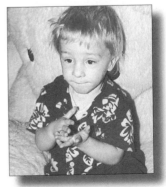

"The next signs we tried were <u>stop</u> and <u>share</u>, which we used when we encountered unacceptable behavior, such as snatching a toy from another child or a more physical act such as pushing, biting or hitting. If a child causes another to cry we teach the sign for <u>hurt</u> and <u>sad</u> or <u>cry</u>, then talk about feelings — we follow up by having the guilty party sign <u>sorry</u>."

Ulrike and staff have observed that over time this sort of behaviour has decreased considerably and it is not unusual to see toddlers sorting out a situation

Adam signs SHARE

themselves by signing <u>stop</u> or <u>wait</u> to their peers instead of reacting by pushing or striking out.

"The <u>work</u> sign was an unexpected favorite with toddlers and we found it helped them to settle better when they had a sign they could use to say where their mother or father had gone. Instead of just looking at the door they sign that <u>Daddy</u> has gone in the <u>car</u> to <u>work</u>. It seemed to help being able to label the whereabouts of important people in their lives. We also found that they liked to tell us about their pets, so naturally these signs were taught and reinforced throughout their day. The children even began to tell us that their <u>dog</u> or <u>cat</u> was at <u>home</u> when asked."

Up and Running with Baby Sign Language

"It wasn't long before the children started to use the signs amongst themselves. Once they discovered they could communicate with each other as well, the signing took off even more!

"It was interesting to watch how each child responded to the use of signs. Some children were real perfectionists and would practice their signs in private before using them in front of anyone else. One little girl (18 months) didn't seem very interested in learning to sign at all — she would turn away whenever I tried to show her a sign. She would watch from a distance when we signed with other children and occasionally used a couple of signs with staff. Due to her lack of interest we didn't push signs on her. You can imagine my surprise when I observed her at play one afternoon and counted her using over 30 signs with her playmates!

"After a few months of using baby sign language we noticed a marked difference in the center. Firstly, the whole atmosphere seemed to change. Noise levels dropped, babies and toddlers cried less often and seemed much more content, and they also interacted with each other and staff more. As teachers we find it so much easier to work with a group of babies who can express their needs and ideas so freely. It has really removed a great deal of frustration and guesswork for us.

"We found that being able to communicate using signs had a marked effect in other areas of the children's development, with a visible improvement in their confidence and self-esteem. Previously quiet or shy toddlers began to come out of their shells more and could stand up for themselves.

"We also noticed that children started to take charge of their own education. By having the ability to communicate using signs, they can tell us exactly what interests them most and are able to extract more information from us. They are very keen to learn about many different topics and on a much deeper level than before. We now find that a far greater percentage of our 20-month-old toddlers are ready to move to the over-twos group. These toddlers are much more verbal, self-sufficient, knowledgeable and capable than our previous nonsigning groups."

Ulrike's Tips for Introducing Baby Sign Language to Your Under-Twos Group

🖐 *For very young babies, start with the sign for <u>milk</u>.*

🖐 *Use a fun action song to introduce a few animal signs (use noises too).*

🖐 *Once the children understand a few basic signs you can begin to introduce the more abstract ideas such as <u>wait</u>, <u>share</u>, <u>please</u> and <u>thank you</u>.*

🖐 *Observe individual children to see what is important to them and introduce signs accordingly.*

🖐 *Be observant and praise any attempt at signing. Expect early signs to be rough approximations of the signs you are teaching.*

🖐 *Simply use baby sign language naturally throughout the day.*

Adam signs APPLAUSE

Dad's Corner — Dad's Role in Signing

By Giles Warburton

Becoming a father for the first time was both an exciting and an emotional time, and being fairly inexperienced with small babies it was also quite daunting. Isabella seemed so tiny and fragile when she first arrived, although she was a whopping nine pounds!

Isabella signs TEDDY

Every parent wants to do the best for their children and I am no exception, but I have to admit that I was very sceptical of baby sign language when Karyn first suggested that we use it with our own baby. Looking back, I felt I didn't have the energy to learn something new, particularly as we were still recovering from months of sleepless nights caused by Isabella's reflux. Fortunately for us, Karyn persevered without me.

The breakthrough came with Isabella's first sign at about nine and a half months. I have to admit to being taken aback at seeing my little baby using the <u>where</u> sign. I hadn't really expected a great deal in the way of communication until much later, and like most parents was overjoyed just to see smiles, hear laughter and try to understand the various grunts and cries. But here for the first time was a clear attempt at communication, and the feeling of intense pleasure from Issy at being understood was easy to see. As you can imagine I instantly became the biggest baby signing fan! It was a case of "Okay, stand back — Dad will take over from here!" It felt almost as if Isabella and I were feeding off each other's excitement as we quickly moved on to other signs, such as <u>more</u>, <u>finished</u>, <u>cat</u>, <u>eat</u>, <u>light</u>, <u>baby</u>, <u>dog</u> and <u>bath</u>.

At first it just looked like too much effort and dedication was needed, but in reality it had just taken a slight adjustment in thinking, and remembering to use our agreed signs whenever we were with Isabella. Within 10 weeks of seeing the first sign repeated, we counted that Issy had about 25 signs and 10 spoken words. This meant that we could "talk" about 35 things together, knowing that the other would understand. This might not sound like much, but we were having so much fun doing it and, above all, Issy seemed to be revelling in the extra attention and praise that came with signing. It made my day when I came home from work in the evening and Issy would tell me she wanted a <u>cuddle</u> or to read a <u>book</u>, have a <u>bath</u> or play with her <u>ball</u>. I had never realized just how much a young baby was capable of understanding.

The comment I hear most from our signing dads is that teaching baby sign language gave them an additional role to play in their baby's lives. One of the reasons that fathers are so vital in teaching signs is that they provide some variety to the learning process for their baby. Lots of the dads I speak to love to do the animated and noisy signs. It is also interesting to see how your baby responds differently to each parent and knows which signs work best with each person. I was surprised at how cunning Isabella could be — she would often sign <u>please</u> with a really cute smile when she wanted a candy from me. She would normally do this immediately after Karyn had just said "No" to her request.

Isabella signs BALL

I found that I had some catching up to do each day when I returned home from work. It wasn't long before night-time routines started to develop around signing, as Isabella would request her favorite songs, games and books just before bed. Signing gave a real purpose to our play, as I could integrate our starter signs into everything we did in those brief times during the week.

24/7 — Using All Available Time

Like most working moms and dads, you may not get to spend a huge amount of time with your baby during the working week. On average, I had 30 minutes in the morning and one to two hours in the evening, and I found I needed to work out a way to maximize this learning time. Luckily for me, we found that first thing in the morning and last thing at night just happened to be the times when our daughter wanted to tell us lots of things, and would begin signing frantically. The excitement of waking up and seeing the birds in the trees through her bedroom window would prompt the associated signs, closely followed by the signs for <u>drink</u>, <u>eat</u>, <u>bath</u> and <u>work</u>. Of course, there were some mornings when Isabella would wake up grumpy and crying, but most of the time I was met with an excited little grin, coupled with the sign for <u>tree</u> or <u>bird</u>, meaning that she wanted me to open the blinds and for us to look out the window.

I'm Awake! — Signing Frenzies

As soon as Isabella knew it was time for bed the evening's signing frenzy would start. It quickly became obvious that this was just a baby ploy to try to convince us that she was not tired at all — "Hey look at me! I can't possibly be tired. Look what I can do with my hands. I still have plenty of energy!"

To put this time to good use, we worked out a simple routine incorporating lots of animal pictures on her bedroom wall. Each bedtime we would spend five to ten minutes going around the room saying good night to them all. Issy would watch intently as I did the signs and repeated the words and animal noises to her. I can still clearly recall the look of fascination as her big eyes would stare at my hands, waiting for the next sign as we talked about <u>tigers</u>, <u>crocodiles</u>, <u>giraffes</u>, <u>zebras</u> and other exciting animals. It wasn't long before she was making the sounds along with me, and shortly after that she started the <u>lion</u> sign, accompanied by an almighty baby "ROAR!" As the weeks progressed, Isabella began to take over and would perform the sign or say the word to me as we looked at each picture. If I was tired and tried to hurry the process by skipping a few of the animals, Issy would instantly demand that we go back to the missed animal.

Isabella signs CAT

Hey Dad, Look at That! — Sharing Your Baby's World

It is so easy to forget that a baby is seeing and experiencing *everything* for the first time, so life is just one big ball of excitement! They want you to tell them what they see and in turn want to tell you when they see something familiar. I remember when we first taught the sign for <u>cat</u>, Isabella was seeing cats everywhere, on posters, in books, on cans of pet food in the supermarket; even a pair of cat earrings worn by a shop assistant was pointed out with great delight. Most of the time I hadn't even noticed these things, it was only seeing Isabella use her sign and "meow" like a cat that made me stop and take a closer look!

I Can Do It! — Greater Independence

Giving your baby the gift of independence not only helps them gain in confidence but also makes them much stronger individuals. By introducing signs for concepts such as <u>help</u>, you are letting them try things out for themselves, knowing you are there to help them out should they need you.

I can still remember the first time Issy used the sign <u>help</u>; she was 15 months old at the time. I had taken her down to the beach by our house, and when we had finished playing, she insisted on climbing back up the makeshift steps from the beach to the road. She struggled her way up the first three steps but couldn't climb up the fourth as it was just too high. After a few moments I impatiently leant forward to pick her up, and as I did, I noticed her using the sign for <u>help</u>. I slowly put my arms out on either side of her and she grabbed my hands and hauled herself up the step with a big grunt. All the while she was still facing forward with a determined look on her face. Once she was over this hurdle, she carried on climbing up the remaining steps. All this was done with no fuss and without a word being said.

I was utterly amazed at this simple situation, purely because I could see how signing was helping to strengthen my baby daughter's feeling of independence. From previous experience I had learned that intervening too early would cause a major tantrum. This is one sign we could not have lived without!

Rough and Tumble — Bring Out the Child in You

Don't be afraid to be loud and animated with your signing (maybe not so much in public places, but really go wild at home!). If you make the learning process fun and engaging for your baby they will pick up the signs very quickly. I personally loved all the animal signs and the more I rolled on the floor and growled like a lion or crowed like a rooster the more Issy wanted to play. The added benefit of teaching these signs is that you have real living subjects to work with. We made regular trips to a children's farm in our neighborhood as this allowed Isabella to get really close to and in some cases actually touch the animals. This let her gain a fuller experience to associate the signs with. We found that signs like pig, mouse, cow, chicken and horse were picked up very quickly because of these frequent visits. It wasn't long before Isabella was busy telling us about the animals she could see on posters, on clothing, in magazines and on television.

It Takes Two — Working with Your Partner on Routines

It helps if you discuss signs you plan to introduce with your partner, mainly because your baby may well already be using them when you are not around.

It also helps if you are fairly consistent with your daily routines. For example, I always used to give Isabella her bath in the morning and knew which new signs to introduce and which ones to reinforce. This is probably most important in the early stages of teaching signs as it will help you gauge how you are progressing. Once your baby has a larger repertoire of signs, you will find that they will tell you what they want to learn about, and so the routines become less important.

Signing and Children with Down Syndrome

With Sharon Eastwood

There are many things a parent can do to help their baby with Down Syndrome in their language development.

Why Is Learning and Producing Spoken Language So Difficult for our Children?

As with all infants, no two babies with Down Syndrome are the same, so naturally they will develop at different rates and a great deal depends on what other health problems your child has to cope with.

- *A baby with Down Syndrome generally learns and develops at a slower rate.*

- *Having low muscle tone and shorter arms and legs makes movement more challenging.*

- *A large majority of children with Down Syndrome also have hearing problems, which in turn make discriminating between similar sounds and words difficult.*

- *A poor verbal memory means it is not easy recalling and organizing specific words and understanding concepts.*

- *Producing speech is difficult due to the low muscle tone of the face and shape and size of the tongue.*

Current research findings suggest that a baby with Down Syndrome finds it difficult to learn "through their ears" and much better able to learn, understand and use language if you concentrate on helping them learn "through their eyes." This can be done with the use of sign language. By concentrating on introducing an alternative mode to produce language, you can make the most of any strengths rather than consistently trying to improve on weaknesses. When you introduce an alternative such as sign language that is physical and visual, you can work alongside the auditory

Ashleigh signs RABBIT

weakness and improve on it gradually as your child grows in confidence. Signing also has the advantage over the spoken word as each sign "can be held static as a model to imitate. Hands can be moulded and shaped into signs far more easily than sounds can be shaped into words" (Grove 1986).

Sharon Eastwood, mother to lively four-year-old Ashleigh, began to sign with her daughter at the age of eight weeks. *"I wanted to do something useful for Ashleigh that would help her in her development of language. I knew that her speech would be delayed so was determined my daughter would not become frustrated at being unable to communicate her needs, thoughts and ideas. I would sign and verbalize words that were important to Ashleigh and would repeat these often throughout our day so that our whole family got involved. As Ashleigh grew we began to notice her watching us intently as we signed, and at the age of six months we were rewarded with her first sign — it was very exciting!"*

Ashleigh's health problems have meant she has needed to spend a great deal of time in the hospital, so Sharon felt it very important to teach her the signs for <u>doctor</u>, <u>nurse</u> and <u>hospita</u>l. *"Some of the medical staff began to pick up on Ashleigh's signs and started to sign back to her as well, which she thought was great. There is an emergency helicopter at the hospital, which Ashleigh found very exciting and of course this sign was an instant hit."*

Ashleigh signs BOOK

Because children with Down Syndrome are generally less responsive, the tendency can be to interact less, offering fewer instances to hear verbal language. *"We made a point of talking constantly to Ashleigh about what we were doing, kind of like a running commentary as the day unfolded. As a result she could see that communication was an important part of our lives and wanted to be included more and more. The more repetition of words and signs Ashleigh received the easier it became for her to remember and use them herself. Because we always encouraged spoken language in conjunction with the signs we noticed that Ashleigh would always attempt to use her voice when she signed. The use of signs really helped us because we knew exactly what she was trying to say and could repeat the word back to her, giving positive reinforcement. This encouraged Ashleigh to keep trying and really gave her confidence a boost because we could understand her."*

There are so many signing systems around now that it can be confusing looking for a place to start. Sharon found that signing worked best for their family if it was kept as simple as possible, and the more iconic the sign the better. The Eastwood family opted to use what worked best for them, which included a mix of Signed English, Australasian Signs, and signs they created themselves.

"We knew what real progress we had made when Ashleigh began to make up her own signs for objects and we happily adopted these in to our own signing vocabulary and this made the process even more fun. You have to be open to your child's inventions because this shows a deep understanding of the process involved and is a wonderful cognitive milestone. It was a great feeling when we were out and people would comment what a clever child Ashleigh was because she had a skill that most children her own age didn't have — she could talk with her hands!

"It wasn't all easy, though. Teaching anything new takes time and patience, but the rewards are well worth the effort. Ashleigh still forgets some signs. I can remember on one occasion Ashleigh wanted to ask for water, but couldn't recall the correct sign. After a couple of 'false starts' she signed <u>wash hands</u>. I was so impressed with her logic!"

Sharon's Signing Tips

- The most important first step is to give your baby plenty of love and attention. Above all else, your baby needs to feel safe and secure in their environment.

- Be sensitive to your child's own abilities.

- Concentrate on what your child can do rather than what they cannot.

- Start small. Don't overwhelm your child with too many signs.

- Sign and speak slowly to allow your child to see and hear what you are doing more easily.

- Help your child to form their hands into the correct shapes when showing them a sign. This way they can feel the sign/word and may help to build up a mental image of the object in question.

- Introduce signs that are fun and of interest to your child, such as animals and favorite toys. Also include signs for important everyday words like drink, eat and toilet.

- Repeat the signs often throughout your day. The more repetition the better.

- Never push learning signs on your baby. There will be times when they are not interested or are too tired.

- Keep the process enjoyable. Ashleigh loved looking at picture books so we made good use of this quiet time together to introduce new signs and reinforce old ones. Action songs were another favorite.

- Make ordinary life something to talk about.

- Ashleigh learned best when taking part in real life experiences rather than lessons.

"Remember that your child's signs will probably look very different to what you have shown them. This is completely normal and any attempts at signing should be rewarded with plenty of praise and encouragement."

For further information about Down Syndrome go to www.ndss.org.

Chapter 8

Signing Dictionary

Signing Index

Milk	105	Rhinoceros	88	Teacher	113
Mine	119	Rooster	138	Teddy bear	133
Minister	112	Rubbish/Trash	144	Telephone	133
Mirror	133	Run	124	Thank you	121
Monkey	88	Sad	117	Tidy	119
Moon	92	Sand/Sandbox	125	Tiger	89
More	140	Sandwich	106	Toilet	128
Mother	112	Sauce	106	Toothbrush	129
Motorcycle	100	Sausages	106	Tractor	100
Mouse	137	School	97	Trailer	100
Music	124	See-saw	125	Train	101
Nappy/Diaper change	140	Share	120	Trash	144
		Shave	128	Tree	93
No	119	Sheep	138	Trousers	85
Noisy	144	Shirt/T-Shirt	84	Truck	101
Nurse	112	Shoes	85	Turtle	138
Orange	106	Shopping	97	Uncle	113
Outside	96	Shorts	85	Underwear	85
Pacifier	132	Shower	128	Up	141
Pain	117	Sing	125	Wait	141
Paint	124	Sister	113	Walk	126
Pajamas	84	Sit down	120	Want	141
Park	97	Sleep	117	Wash face	129
Pig	137	Slide	125	Wash hair	129
Pirate	112	Small	145	Wash hands	129
Play	124	Snail	93	Watch	134
Playground	97	Snake	89	Water	107
Play-Doh	124	Socks	85	Where	141
Please	119	Sorry	120	Wind	94
Policeman	112	Speak	120	Window	145
Present	144	Spider	93	Work	97
Priest	112	Stars	93	Worm	94
Quiet	120	Stop	141	Yours	121
Rabbit	138	Sun	93	Yuk!	143
Rain	92	Sweet/Lollipop	107	Zebra	89
Rainbow	92	Swimming	125	Zoo	97
Raisins	106	Swing	126		

Sign Grading

We have categorized the signs in order to assist you with choosing signs appropriate to your baby's developmental stages. The age ranges are intended as a guide only.

🖐 Ages 0–9 months

🖐 🖐 Ages 9–13 months

🖐 🖐 🖐 Ages 14+ months

Isabella signs a very animated HORSE

Clothing

Luke signs HAT

Coat

Clench fists and place at chest level, with knuckles touching. Swing formation outwards (180 degrees), as if opening a coat.

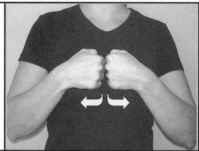

Dress

Hands raised, fingers flexed so that forefingers point up and backs of fingers touch the chest. Brush the backs of fingers from chest to waist level, finishing with all fingers pointing downward, in a sweeping motion.

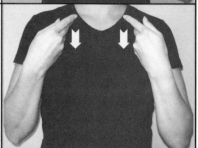

Hat

Pat the top of your head with the palm of your dominant hand.

Pajamas

Brush fingertips of open hand down and up chest.

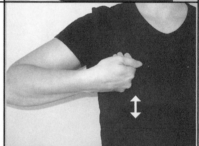

Shirt/T-Shirt

With thumb and index fingers of both hands, gently tug at collar on either side of your neck.

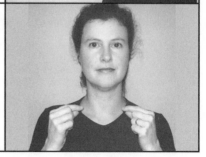

Shoes

Touch your fists together several times.

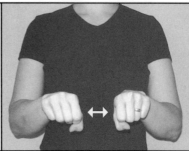

Shorts

Run the blade of your open hand across your thigh.

Socks

Place thumbs into crooked index fingers, palms facing forward. Swivel the formation from the wrist toward your body, as if pulling on a sock.

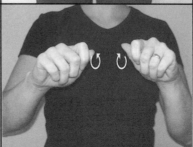

Trousers

Make a *C* shape with your thumb and index finger. Place at waist level and move formation downward.

Underwear

Place lightly clenched fists at mid-thigh level and move formation upward, as if pulling on a pair of pants.

Wild Animals

Garth signs MONKEY

Bear

With arms crossed, lightly scratch your upper chest.

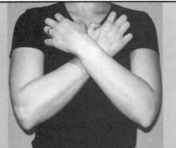

Crocodile

With arms joined at elbows and palms of hands touching together, open and close formation to the elbow, as if a snapping crocodile.

Elephant

Place your fist with index finger extended on to your nose, as if it were an elephant's trunk. Make elephant noises (if you know how!).

Giraffe

With dominant hand in a *C* shape, move your hand from the bottom of your neck upward, indicating a long giraffe neck.

Gorilla

Pound your chest with clenched fists.

Hippopotamus

Make two fists and join them together at the wrists, palms facing. Open and close formation to represent a hippopotamus's mouth.

Kangaroo

Pat your tummy to represent a kangaroo's pouch.

Alternatively, bounce like a kangaroo.

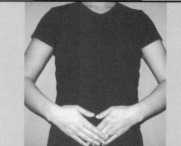

Lion

Move your hands in front of you like a lion clawing and make lion noises.

Monkey

Scratch your armpits like a monkey and make monkey noises.

Rhinoceros

Extend thumb and little finger and place thumb on nose.

Snake

Move your arm as though it were a slithering snake. Make hissing noises.

Tiger

With fingers apart and palms facing cheeks, pull fingers across, but not touching you face, to represent stripes.

Zebra

Make a claw shape with your hand and drag the formation from your shoulder diagonally across your chest, to represent stripes.

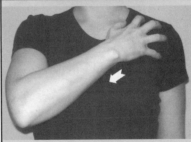

In the Garden/
Outside

Alyx signs FLOWERS

Bee

With thumb and forefinger in a pincher grip, move your hand around like a flying bee. Make buzzing sounds.

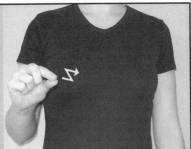

Bird

Flap both your arms like a bird's wings.

Butterfly

Hold open hands palms down, touching at the thumbs. Wave your fingers as if they were flapping wings.

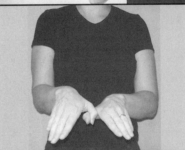

Caterpillar

Bend and straighten your index finger as though it were a caterpillar moving along.

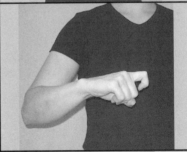

Clouds

Hold your hand above your head with fingers spread and slightly curved. Twist your hand at the wrist, as if screwing in a lightbulb.

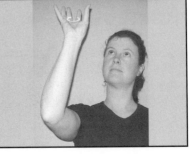

Flower

Hold your fist to your nose and sniff loudly, as if smelling a flower.

Fly

With your hands held up in front of you, make little flapping movements with your fingers to indicate little wings.

Moon

Form a *C* shape with your hand and hold it up above your head.

Rain

With both hands above your head, wiggle your fingers as you move your hands downward.

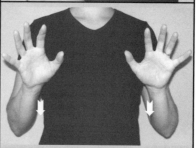

Rainbow

Hold open hand in front of your body at chest height. Move formation in an arc from left to right.

Snail

Crook your index fingers and place them at your temples to represent a snail's antennae.

Spider

Hold your hand in front of you and wiggle your fingers like a spider's legs.

Stars

Hold your hands in the air above your head with fingers apart and wiggling.

Sun

Hold your hand above your head with all fingertips touching. Now open your hand and spread your fingers apart.

Tree

Lightly wave your arm to represent a tree waving in the wind.

Wind

Twirl your forearm in a circular motion to represent a whirlwind. Blow on your baby's face so they can feel the sensation of wind.

Worm

Wiggle your extended index finger up and down (keeping it straight).

Places to Go

Luke signs OUTSIDE

Beach

Move your open hand up and down across the front of your body, as if it were a wave on the ocean.

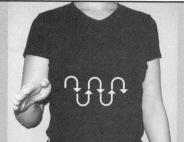

Church

Place palms together as if praying.

Farm

With open hands touching at thumbs and palms facing downward, move formation apart.

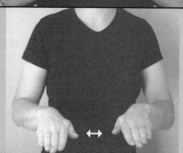

Home

Form the shape of a roof with your hands.

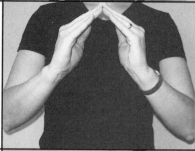

Outside

Move your hand away from your body in a forward movement.

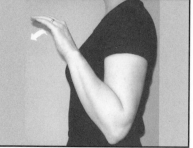

Park/Playground

Tap the thumb side of your open hand against your shoulder several times.

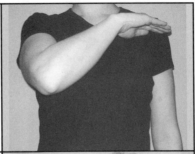

School

Place open right hand diagonally in front of your face. Move formation forward and back slightly twice, as if saluting.

Shopping

Pretend to push a shopping cart along.

Work

Tap the sides of your open hands together crossways.

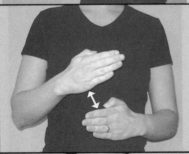

Zoo

Hold your hands up in front of your chest in a slight claw shape. Bend both hands downward from the wrist and up again a few times.

Transport

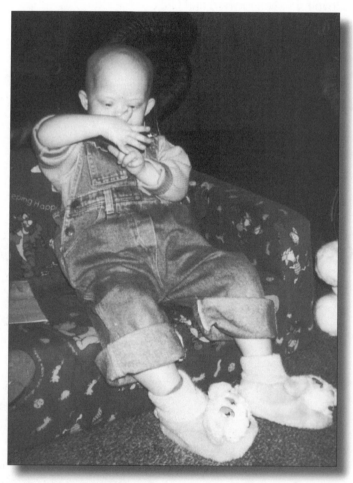

Ashleigh signs HELICOPTER

Airplane

With thumb and little finger extended, move your hand upward, simulating a flying plane.

Ambulance

Hold a clenched fist at ear level. Open and close your hand to represent a flashing light.

Bicycle

Move your clenched fists in a forward circular motion, as though they were the pedals on a bicycle.

Boat

Touch the fingertips of both hands together to form the shape of the bow of a boat. Move the formation forward.

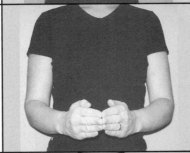

Bus

Pretend to be holding the sides of a large bus steering wheel and move hands in a circular motion.

Car

Move your hands as if you are holding a steering wheel. Make car sounds.

Helicopter

Extend index finger of right hand. Left hand is open with fingers spread, palm facing down. Place the left hand formation on top of your extended finger.

Motorcycle

Pretend to be holding on to the handlebars of a motorbike and twist the right hand as if revving the engine. Make motorcycle noises.

Tractor

Crook and spread fingers of both hands in front of chest. Twist formations from the wrist twice.

Trailer

Bend right index finger and hook over fingertips of cupped left hand. Move formation left to right at chest level.

Train

Move your arms like the wheels of a locomotive.

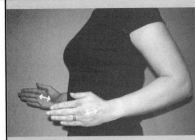

Truck

Bend fingers of right hand and place fingertips at 90 degree angle against open left hand, about halfway down. Move entire formation to the left as if a truck and trailer.

Food

Seb signs COOKIE

Apple

Form a *C* shape with right hand. With palm facing chin, tilt the formation upward from the wrist as if eating an apple.

Banana

With your index finger of one hand pointing upward, pretend to peel this finger using your other hand.

Biscuit/Cookie

Have one hand flat and make a claw shape with the other. Rotate the claw-shaped hand on the open palm of the other, as if opening a cookie jar.

Bread

Move the blade of open right hand against the open left hand, as if slicing bread.

Breast-feed

Use your dominant hand to pat lightly on your upper chest.

Butter

Move fingertips of right hand along palm of open left hand in an upward motion, twice.

Cake

Bounce tips of fingers and thumb of cupped right hand on back of left hand.

Cereal

Cup left hand at chest level, as if a bowl. Mime holding a spoon in right hand and proceed to scoop cereal toward your mouth and back down to "bowl" in a circular motion, twice.

Cheese

Left hand open, palm facing upward. Right hand open, fingertips above open left hand, thumb tucked in. Move right hand backward and forward across flat left hand.

Chips

Make a triangle shape with index fingers and thumbs of both hands touching. Move formation apart while closing tips together.

Drink

Form your hand as if holding a cup and pretend to drink from it.

Eat

Tap the fingers and thumb of your dominant hand to your lips repeatedly.

Egg

Extend right index finger. Move finger along left index finger and up the side of the thumb.

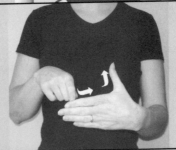

Ice cream

Pretend you are holding an ice cream cone and lick it. (You can do the movement without poking your tongue out if you prefer!)

Milk

Open and close your extended hand, as if you are milking a cow.

Orange

Hold relaxed right fist at right corner of mouth. Clench fist twice.

Raisins

Fingers and thumb of left hand should be touching, leaving a hollow through the middle of the formation. Right hand forms a pincher and moves in and out of left hand hollow.

Sandwich

Hold both hands with fingers and thumbs opposed (as if holding a sandwich), at chin level.

Sauce

Make a *C* shape with your hand and mime shaking sauce from a bottle in a downward motion.

Sausages

Make fists with both hands, touching with palms down. Open and close hands slightly while moving apart, as if creating a string of sausages.

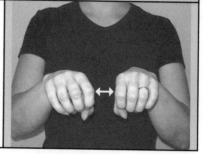

Sweet/Lollipop

Touch your cheek with your index finger and twist your hand back and forth from the wrist.

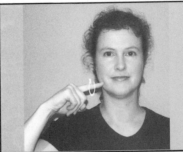

Water

Tap the first three extended fingers of your dominant hand against your lips a few times.

People

Isabella signs BABY

Aunt

Form fists with thumbs extended, knuckles facing. Tap thumbs together twice.

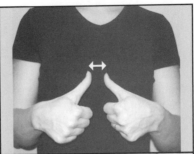

Baby/Doll

Rock your arms side to side as if cradling a baby.

Boy

Move your extended index finger sideways across your chin.

Brother

Form fists with both hands. Rub the formation up and down twice.

Clown

Crook the fingers of your dominant hand and place the formation over your nose.

Doctor

Place extended right thumb and index and middle fingers on the left wrist, with the thumb positioned on the underside of the wrist, as if feeling for a pulse.

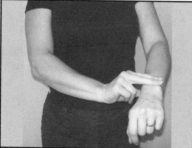

Family

Place open right hand, fingers slightly spread, palm downward at chest level. Move formation in an counter-clockwise circle.

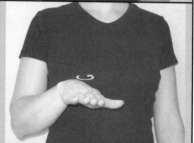

Father

Crook the index finger on your dominant hand and tap the side of your chin.

Fireman

Form fists with both hands. Place one fist in front of the other, palms up, as if holding a fire hose. Move formation from side to side.

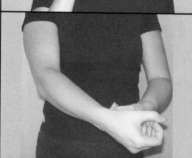

Friend

With one hand wrapped around the other, move hands forward and back in front of your chest several times.

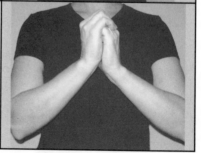

Girl

Lightly smooth your cheek with the index finger of your dominant hand.

Grandfather

Bang clenched fists together, one on top of the other, followed by the sign for <u>father</u>. Alternatively, just use the first half of the sign or create your own.

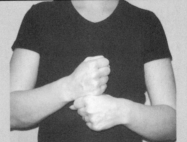

Grandmother

Bang clenched fists together, one on top of the other, followed by the sign for <u>mother</u>. Alternatively, just use the first half of the sign or create your own.

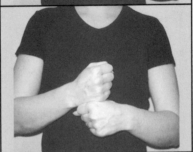

Lady

Move the fingertips of open right hand down the right cheek.

Man

Clench right fist under your chin and move formation downward.

Mother

Extend the index finger of your dominant hand and tap your temple.

Nurse

Form a *C* shape with thumb and forefinger of right hand. Move formation across forehead, right to left.

Pirate

Place open hand over one eye, as if an eye-patch.

Policeman

With both fists clenched and fingers facing downward, cross formation as if wearing handcuffs.

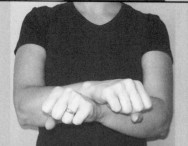

Priest/Minister

Form a *C* with thumb and index finger of right hand. Move the formation across the neck from left to right.

Sister

Crook your right index finger and tap formation on bridge of nose twice.

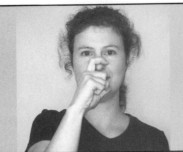

Teacher

Extend right index finger and place formation in front of right side of head. Move formation forward and backward twice.

Uncle

Extend little fingers, palms facing body. Tap little fingers together twice.

Feelings/ Emotions

Isabella signs SLEEPING — i.e., the dog is sleeping

Angry

Make a claw shape with your dominant hand and hold it up to your face. Make an angry face and slowly pull hand outward and down, curling your fingers as you do so. Stomp your foot for extra effect!

Bad dream

Tap the side of your head with the fingertips of your dominant hand.

Cold

Clench your fists and hold them up at shoulder level. Hunch your shoulders and shiver as if cold.

Cry

Make a sad face and use index fingers to trace tears down your cheeks. Make crying noises.

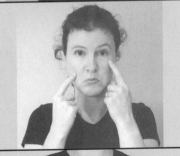

Cuddle/Hug

Hug your arms across your chest and swivel your shoulders slightly.

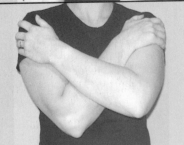

Frightened

Gasp and hold both your hands, fingers curled, up to your chin as if biting your fingernails.

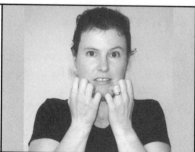

Gentle

Gently stroke the back of one hand with the fingertips of the other.

Good

Clench both fists and raise both thumbs.

Happy

Use your dominant hand to lightly brush the middle of your chest in an upward motion.

Hot

Shake your dominant hand in front of your body at chest level, as if you have just burnt your finger. Make blowing sounds.

Hurt/Pain

Tap your index fingers together repeatedly at the area where the pain is occurring.

Love

With one open hand over the other, place formation over your heart.

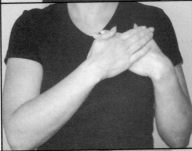

Sad

Place your open dominant hand sideways at the center of your face (thumb side in). Slowly move the formation downward. Make a sad face.

Sleep

Place your hands together at the side of your cheek and make snoring sounds.

Manners/ Commands

Adam signs PLEASE

Clean/Tidy

Rub your open palm with your clenched fist in a circular motion.

Don't touch/No

Clap your hands together sharply while shaking your head and saying "no" or "don't touch."

Listen/Hear

Cup your hand behind your ear.

Mine

Make a fist and bang it on your chest several times.

Please

Place your open hand on your chest and rub in a circular motion.

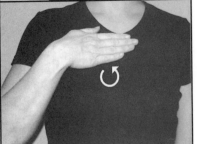

Quiet

Place an index finger on your lips and say "ssssh."

Share

Pretend to divide up a cake by making a chopping motion down the palm of your other hand.

Sit down

Place one hand on top of the other and push down.

Sorry

Make a fist with your thumb extended and rub your chest in a circular motion.

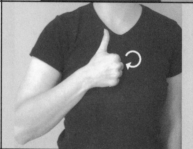

Speak

Place tip of index finger at corner of mouth and move outwards, away from your face, twice.

Thank you

Start by touching your fingertips to your chin and then move them away from your face in an outward motion.

Yours

Make a fist with right hand and, with palm facing away from you, move formation forward.

Activities/ Games

Isabella signs SWING

Blocks

Make fists with both hands and place one on top of the other. Move fist from bottom of formation and place on the top. Repeat twice.

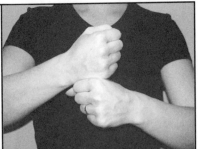

Dance

Pretend that your outstretched fingers are a persons legs and "dance" them on the palm of your other hand.

Fall down

Place index and middle fingers of dominant hand onto the palm of other hand. Now make fingers "fall" off your open palm.

Hide

Cover your face with your hands.

Kite

Hold your open hand with palm facing outward at shoulder height. Zigzag the formation upward to represent a kite flying.

Music

Wave both your index fingers in the air as if you are a conductor.

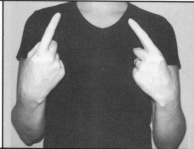

Paint

Use your open right hand in an up-and-down sweeping motion, as if it were a paintbrush.

Play

With both hands open and palms facing upward, make circular movements with your hands.

Play-Doh

At chest level, pretend to knead dough by slightly opening and closing your hands.

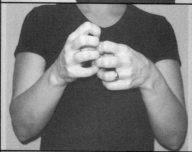

Run/Chase me

Move your arms as if running.

Sand/Sandbox

Rub the fingertips on each hand together as if sprinkling sand.

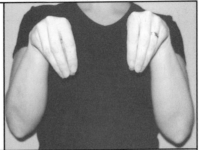

See-saw

Hold your hands out in front of you and alternately raise and lower them as if they were a see-saw.

Sing

Starting with your index finger touching your lips, spiral it outward, away from your face.

Slide

Start with your hands side by side at chest level and then swoop them downward and outward from your body, as if going down a slide.

Swimming

Pretend to be swimming the breaststroke.

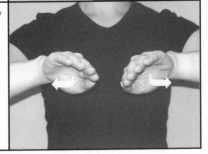

Swing

Swing your bent arms back and forth at waist level.

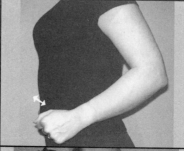

Walk

"Walk" index and middle fingers of dominant hand across the palm of other hand.

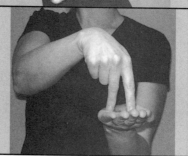

In the Bathroom

Isabella signs TOOTHBRUSH

Bath

Rub your closed fists on your chest as if washing yourself.

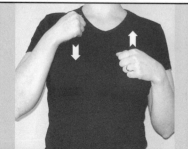

Hair/Hairbrush

Act as if brushing your hair with your fingers.

Shave

Pretend you are holding a razor and move the formation across the jawline.

Shower

Bounce lightly cupped hand above head.

Toilet

Tug your earlobe using your thumb and forefinger.

Toothbrush

Rub your index finger against your teeth in a brushing motion.

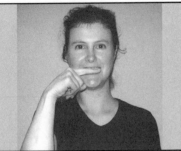

Wash face

Using an open hand, pretend to wash your face in a circular motion.

Wash hair

Using crooked fingers of both hands, pretend to wash your hair.

Wash hands

Act as if washing your hands.

Favorite Objects

Garth signs TELEPHONE

Bag

Hold your lightly clenched hand out in front of you as if you are holding a bag.

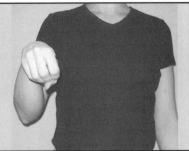

Ball

Tap all your fingers together to indicate a ball shape.

Book

Open and close your hands as if they are a book.

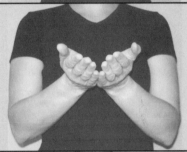

Bubbles

Alternate opening and closing your hands as if they are bubbles popping.

Camera

Make the shape of a camera with your hands in front of your face. Pretend to take a picture by pressing the button and making a clicking sound.

Baby Sign Language

Candle

Pretend your index finger is a candle and pretend to blow out the flame.

Clock

Make a fist with one hand and extend your index finger. Place this hand onto the open palm of your other hand and rotate as if the hands of a clock.

Computer

With your hands out in front of you, move your fingers as if typing on a computer keyboard.

Crab

Thumb and index fingers of both hands pinch together as if they are a crab's claws.

Dummy/Pacifier

Place forefinger and thumb against your lips as if putting in a pacifier.

Fire

With the palms of your hands facing upward, wiggle your fingers to indicate flames.

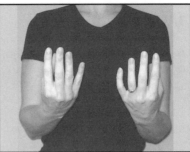

Light

Point your index finger upward then bend it, making a clicking sound as if turning on a switch.

Mirror

Hold your hand in front of your face as if looking in a mirror.

Teddy bear

Lightly scratch your shoulders in a clawing motion.

Telephone

Hold your fist to your ear.

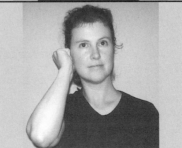

Watch

With index and second fingers together, tap the wrist of your other arm, where your watch is located.

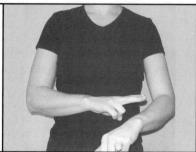

Animals

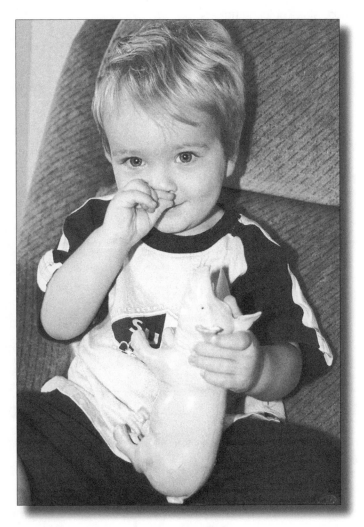

Garth signs PIG

Cat

Stroke your forearm, moving hand downward toward your wrist, as if stroking a cat.

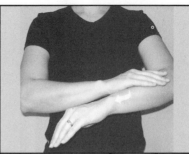

Chicken

Tuck your hands in your armpits and flap your pretend wings. Make chicken noises.

Cow

Place both your fists, with index fingers extended, onto the sides of your head to represent horns. Make lots of mooing noises.

Dog

Pat your thigh several times as if calling a dog.

Duck

With your hand under your chin, open and close your fingers as if they were a duck's beak. Make quacking sounds.

Fish

Wiggle your hand to simulate a fish swimming. Open and close your mouth also.

Frog

With a fist under your chin, extend thumb and index and second finger several times and poke out your tongue. Alternatively, poke out your tongue several times as if catching a fly.

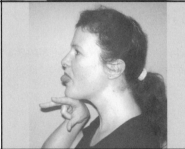

Horse

Move your hands as if holding the reins and riding a horse. Make lots of neighing noises.

Mouse

Gently stroke the sides of your nose with your open hands, as if you are a mouse washing its face.

Pig

Make a fist and place the thumb end onto the end of your nose and twist slightly. Make pig grunting noises.

Rabbit
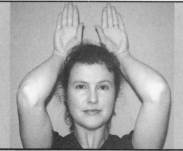

Open both hands and place on top of your head, palms facing forward, like a rabbit's ears.

Rooster

Place your hand on your head with fingers apart and make rooster noises.

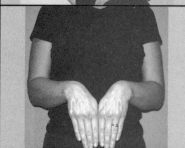

Sheep

Place your hands at waist level side by side so your index fingers are touching. Bounce your hands outward several times, like a skipping lamb.

Turtle

Make a fist with one hand and extend your thumb. Wrap your other hand over the top to form the turtle's shell.

Independence

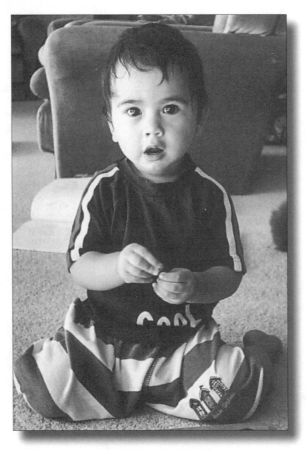

Conrad signs MORE

Down

Point downward repeatedly.

Finished/All gone

Rotate your hands at the wrist in front of your chest.

Help

Pat both hands against your chest repeatedly.

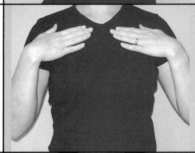

More

Tap the fingers of one hand into the open palm of the other, as if placing an object into your hand.

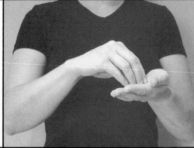

Nappy/Diaper change

Place your hands as if opening the tabs on a disposable diaper.

Stop

Hold your open hand out in front of you as if stopping traffic.

Up

Point upward repeatedly.

Wait

Hold hands up in front of you, palms facing outward, and lightly bounce them, pushing outward.

Want

With the palms of both hands facing upward, make grasping movements with your fingers.

Where

Throw your arms up and shrug your shoulders.

Miscellaneous

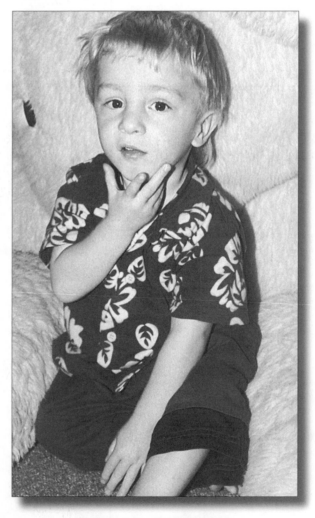

Adam signs CHRISTMAS

Big

Hold both your arms out wide to indicate something large.

Birthday

Bounce tips of fingers and thumb of cupped right hand on back of left hand (same sign as <u>cake</u>).

Broken

Pretend you are holding a stick between two clenched fists and snap it in half.

Christmas

Cup chin with right hand and move formation downward, closing the thumb and fingertips as you do so, twice, as if stroking a long beard.

Dirty/Yuk!

Place one hand at the base of your throat and pretend to retch or say "yuk!"

Door

Place one open hand in front of the other. Move the front hand's fingertips outward, away from the body, as if a door opening.

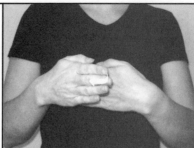

Medicine

Extend right hand little finger and form an *O* shape with left hand. Stir right little finger into left formation.

Noisy

Cup your hands over your ears.

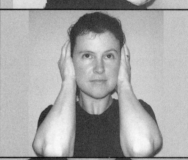

Present/Gift

Roll open hands in forward circles around each other several times.

Rubbish/Trash

Start with a closed fist held up at shoulder height and move hand downward, opening your hand and extending your fingers as you do so, as if throwing something in the garbage.

Small

With hands open and palms facing each other a little distance apart, bounce them toward each other slightly.

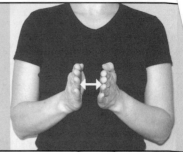

Window

Both hands open, palms facing inward, place hands one on top of the other. Move hands apart, one upward and one downward, then back again, as if opening and closing a window.

References

Bruner, J., (1983) *Child's Talk: Learning to Use Language.* New York: WW Norton and Co.

Corballis, M. C., (2002) *From Hand to Mouth: The Origins of Language.* Princeton University Press.

Daniels, M., (2001) *Dancing With Words: Signing for Hearing Children's Literacy.* Connecticut: Bergin & Garvey.

Einon, D., (1998) *Early Learning.* Sydney: New Holland Publishers.

Hannaford, C. H., (1995) *Smart Moves: Why Learning Is Not All in Your Head.* Alexandria, VA: Great Ocean Publishers.

Wieman, J. M. and R. P. Harrison, eds., (1983) *Nonverbal Interaction.* Beverly Hills: Sage Publications.

Wilson, F., (1999) *The Hand: How It Shapes the Brain, Language and Human Culture.* New York: Vintage Books.

www.baby-talk.com